Vorwort

Das neue 2-bändige **Kickoff** Nordrhein-Westfalen entspricht komplett dem Lehrplan der Ausbildungsvorbereitungsschule und der Berufsfachschule, Typ I und II in Nordrhein-Westfalen.

— Durch die Aufteilung in 2 Bände kann Kickoff – je nach Schulart – folgendermaßen eingesetzt werden:

Kickoff-Band	Schulart	Bildungsziel	Sprachniveau
Kickoff Foundation	Ausbildungsvorbereitungsschule Berufsfachschule Typ I (erstes Jahr)	nachgeholter oder qualifizierter Hauptschulabschluss	Foundation: A2
Kickoff Upgrade	Berufsfachschule Typ I (zweites Jahr) Berufsfachschule Typ II	Qualifizierter Realschulabschluss	Upgrade: B1

— Noch übersichtlicher durch das komplett überarbeitete Layout.
— Zahlreiche Differenzierungsmöglichkeiten zur individuellen Förderung durch neue Texte und Aufgaben mit unterschiedlichem Schwierigkeitsgrad (leicht – mittel – schwer) auf den selektiv ansteuerbaren *More please!*-Seiten.
— Zahlreiche inhaltliche Erweiterungen:
  - Viele zusätzliche Texte und Hörverständnisaufgaben
  - 6 neue Videos zum Training des Seh-/Hörverstehens
  - Alle *Skills* werden mittels *Skills files* ausführlich dargestellt.
  - Berufsspezifische Vertiefung (Wirtschaft & Verwaltung, Technik, Soziales & Gesundheit) durch *Job pages* im Anhang.
— Vertieftes Vokabular- und Grammatiktraining:
  Kickoff Foundation Workbook
  Kickoff Upgrade Workbook
— Im Preis bereits dabei: neues, interaktives Vokabeltraining online und zahlreiche Downloads durch Eingabe von **Kickoff**-Codes auf www.klett.de.

Lernhilfen und Symbole:

Am Ende von Unit 4 kann ich:	Lernziele des Lehrplans	V4	Videoverweis
Tips and tricks!	Sprachtipps für deutsche Lerner	→ Grammar	Verweis auf die Grammatik
Hier und dort	Interkulturelles	P, M, I, R	Produktion, Mediation, Interaktion oder Rezeption
→ (Vokabel)	Die wichtigsten Vokabeln auf der Seite auf einen Blick	2se2hk	Vokabel- und Grammatiktraining online über www.klett.de und Audio-Download (MP3)
→ More please!	Hinweis auf die Differenzierungsseiten	△	Differenzierung nach unten
Video Lounge	authentische Videos	▲	Differenzierung nach oben
A1.27	Audioverweis		

Entry
English, English, everywhere

s37y4x

1 Hi. Do you speak English?

R **A Read about Silke and Robbie. Where are they?**

This weekend, there's a music festival near Cologne. There are bands from Europe and the USA. Lots of young people are at the festival. Silke and Robbie are there too.

R, P **B Listen. Then read their dialogue with a partner.**

A 1.1

Robbie **Silke**

Robbie: Hi. Do you speak English?

Silke: A bit!

Robbie: My name's Robbie.

Silke: Hi. I'm Silke.

Robbie: Where are you from?

Silke: I'm from Dusseldorf in Germany. What about you?

Robbie: I'm from London in England.

P **C You're at the festival too. You meet a young woman called Brooke from Chicago, in the USA. Make a dialogue with your partner. Take it in turns to be Brooke.**

Hi. Do you speak English?

…

P **D Say 'hi' to your class.**

Hi. I'm …
Hello. My name's …

P **E Finish the sentences.**

1 Silke and Robbie … at a music festival.
2 Where … the festival? – It … near Cologne.
3 Robbie … English. He … from London.
4 Where … you from? – I … from Germany.

→ Cologne → lots of → what about you? → to meet
→ to take it in turns → dialogue

Das Verb *to be*

I am (I'm)	I'm not
he is (he's) she is (she's) it is (it's)	he isn't she isn't it isn't
we are (we're) you are (you're) they are (they're)	we aren't you aren't they aren't

Fragen:
*Where **is she** from?*
*Where **are you / they** from?*

Am Ende von Entry habe ich:

— die Basis-Grammatik und den Grundwortschatz des Englischen wiederholt,
— Englisch als Weltsprache kennengelernt.

2 What are their names?

R, P **A** **Lots of people in the world speak English. Where are these native speakers from? How old are they? What are their jobs?**

Marianne is from … She's … (years old). She's a …
Phil, Adam and Lilly are … They're … They're …

Hi. My name's Marianne. I'm 18 and I'm from Canada. I'm a secretary.

Hello. Our names are Phil, Adam and Lilly. We're from Britain and we're all 17. We're students.

Hi. I'm Brandon and I'm from the USA. I'm 22 and I'm a construction worker.

G'day. We're Greg and Georgina. We're nurses and we're from Australia. We're 19.

My name's Gordon. Hi. I'm 21 and I'm a computer technician. I'm from New Zealand.

P, I **B** **What are their names? Ask another student.**

He's 21 and he's a computer technician.
– His name's Gordon.
She's from Canada.
– Her name's …

→ secretary → nurse → technician

P **C** **Read about Hannah and finish the sentences with the words next to the sentences.**

Hannah is Gordon's girlfriend. Gordon is the guy from New Zealand on the last page. This is Hannah's family.

Hannah and her
sister Sophie, 19

dad > Patrick
mum > Emma

brother > Jack, 14

1 Hannah's ... name is Jack. Jack is 14.
2 Her ... name is Sophie. Hannah and Sophie are twins.
3 Her ... name is Patrick. He's a painter and decorator.
4 Her ... name is Emma. ... mum is a doctor's receptionist.

dad's
Hannah's
sister's
brother's
mum's

I **D** **Ask a partner.**

What's your mum's / dad's name?

Do you have a brother or a sister? What are their names?

R, P **E** **What's right: a or b?**

1 This is Marianne. a) *He's* b) *She's* from Canada.
2 He's from the USA. a) *His* b) *Her* name's Brandon.
3 These two people are from Australia.
a) *Her* b) *Their* names are Greg and Georgina.
4 a) *Hannahs* b) *Hannah's* dad is called Patrick.
5 a) *Her* b) *His* mum is called Emma.
6 Hannah and Sophie are a) *Jacks* b) *Jack's* sisters.

→ sentence → receptionist

Genitiv 's

Gordon's girlfriend (Gordons Freundin)
My girlfriend's dad (Der Vater meiner Freundin)

3 A holiday in Montana

R **A Read about Jan.**

1 Where's he from?
2 Where does he want to go this summer?

Jan Wisniewski is from Frankfurt in Germany. Jan likes all sports – walking, cycling, canoeing, football, ... This summer, he wants to go on holiday to Montana.

P, R, I
A 1.2
B Jan wants to go to a hostel in Montana. You can see the hostel brochure on the next page. Jan is on the phone to Matt, the hostel warden.

1 Complete the sentences below with *there's* or *there are*.
2 Listen and check your answers.
3 Read the dialogue with a partner.

Matt **Jan**

Matt: High Mountain Hostel. Matt speaking.

Jan: Hi. My name's Jan. I'm from Germany. I have some questions about the hostel. Is that OK?

Matt: Sure, Jan. What do you want to know?

Jan: How many rooms are there?

Matt: OK. **(1)** *There's* one room for eight people. **(2)** ... two rooms for four people, six rooms for two people and **(3)** ... also four rooms for one person.

Jan: What about facilities?

Matt: Well, **(4)** ... a dining room, **(5)** ... four washing machines, and **(6)** ... two computers. **(7)** ... a TV room – oh, yes, and **(8)** ... a small shop.

Jan: Thanks very much, Matt. That's great.

Matt: You're welcome. Bye.

→ next → (youth) hostel → to go on holiday (to)

Welcome to the High Mountain Hostel

ROOMS

- 1 room for 8 people
- 2 rooms for 4 people
- 6 rooms for 2 people
- 4 rooms for 1 person

FACILITIES

- Dining room (breakfast 7.30, lunch 1.00, evening meal 7.00)
- 4 washing machines
- 2 computers with Internet access
- TV room
- Shop (open 8.00 – 4.00 for snacks, drinks, maps etc.)

CONTACT US

- Phone 271-389 24465
- Website www.highmountainhostel.com

C **It's summer and Jan is at the hostel. He has some questions for Matt about the town. Take it in turns to be Matt and Jan.**

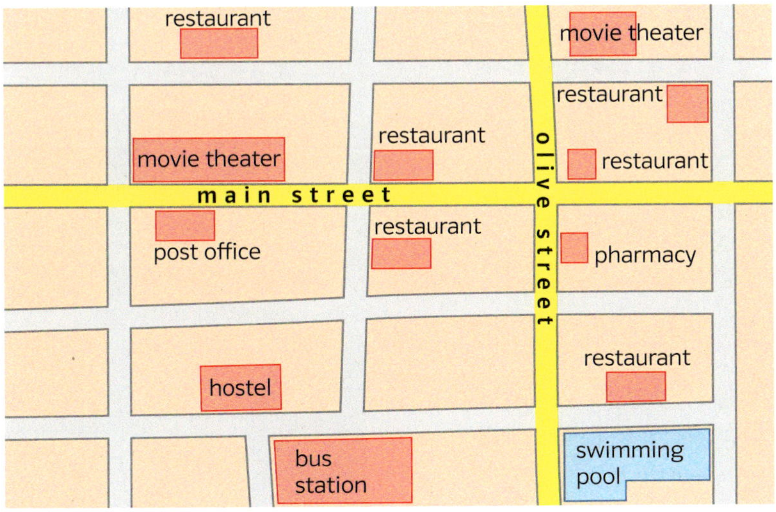

Is there a swimming pool in the town?

Yes. There's a swimming pool here.

Is there a movie theater?

Yes. There are two. Here and here.

→ map → movie theater (US) → main street

There's (is) / there are

There's one dining room.
There are two computers.

4 Rich and famous

A Do you know?

Who are your favourite 'celebs' – famous film stars, sportspeople, singers and musicians – and what do you know about them? Here is a page from a celebrity magazine. Try the quiz!

A QUIZ

MATS HUMMELS

True or false? Write down 'T' or 'F'.

1 Mats Hummels is from Germany.
2 He plays for Germany and Bayern Munich.
3 He is 1.91m tall.
4 He has a younger brother called Erik (also a footballer).
5 He loves computer games – like Wii tennis and playing online games.

LADY GAGA

Which is right? Note down a, b or c.

6 Lady Gaga is from
a Britain. b the USA. c France.
7 Her real name is
a Maria Gaga. b Lady Jane. c Stefani Germanotta.
8 She sings, writes songs and plays
a the piano. b the guitar. c the piano and the guitar.
9 She has 10 tattoos – but where?
a Only the left side of her body. b Only on the right side of her body. c Only on her back.

ROBERT PATTINSON

True or false? Write down 'T' or 'F' again.

10 Robert Pattinson is an actor and was in one of the Harry Potter films.
11 He is from California.
12 He has the middle name 'Jack'.
13 He has an older sister who is in a band.
14 Robert is also a good musician and once played in a band called Bad Girls.

→ musician → band

R, P, I **B Ask a student in your class to read out the answers on page 142. How many right answers do you have? Tell the class.**

I have … right answers.

P, I **C What do you have? Work with a partner.**

1 First copy and fill in the questionnaire for YOU.
2 Ask your partner the questions and fill in your partner's answers.
3 Tell the class about your partner.
Linda / Benjamin has …
(S)he doesn't have …

Which things do you have?	**YOU**	**YOUR PARTNER**
1 brothers and / or sisters	?	?
2 a bike / a car / a motor bike / a scooter / a skateboard / inline skates	?	?
3 a laptop / a smartphone	?	?
4 a tattoo	?	?
5 a Lady Gaga album	?	?
6 a poster of a famous person	?	?
7 a musical instrument (a guitar etc.)	?	?

Do you have brothers and sisters?

Yes, I have …

Do you have a …?

No, I don't have …

P **D Finish the sentences with the correct forms of *to have*.**

1 I … a PC but I … (not) have a laptop.
2 … your friend … a car?
3 He … a motor bike but he … (not) have a car.
4 Lots of film stars … a famous boyfriend or girlfriend.
5 … you … a Lady Gaga album? – No way! I think she's terrible!

Das Verb *to have*	
I have	I don't have
he has she has it has	he doesn't have she doesn't have it doesn't have
we have you have they have	we don't have you don't have they don't have
Fragen: ***Do*** *I / we / you / they* ***have?*** ***Does*** *he / she / it* ***have?***	

→ to fill in (a questionnaire) → read out → smartphone

5 A social networking site

R **A Match the clocks and the times.**

1

2

3

4

5
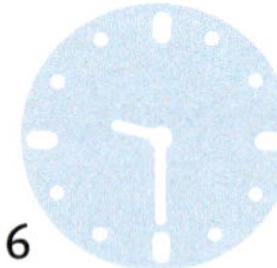
6
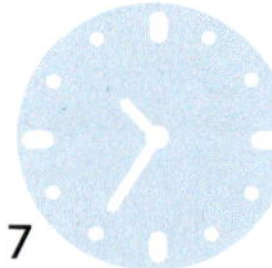
7

8

9

10

1 ten past four
2 ten to one
3 five past three
4 ten o'clock
5 twenty past six
6 twenty-five to eleven
7 half past nine
8 (a) quarter to eleven
9 (a) quarter past eleven
10 12 o'clock / midday / midnight

I, P **B Work with a partner. Point to a clock and ask the time.**

What time is it? – It's …

R **C Julie has written about herself on a social networking site. Listen and note down the missing times.**

A1.3

Hey!

About me

I'm Julie Chang. I'm from New York in the USA.
I'm 20 years old and I work for a fashion company.

My day

I work from Monday to Friday. I get up at **(1)** … Then I jog in the park. At **(2)** … I travel to work on the subway. I start work at **(3)** … I eat my lunch at **(4)** … I go home at **(5)** … I say 'hello' to my friends in my apartment, then I cook my supper.

→ to match → to point to → missing → social networking site → fashion → subway

P **D** **Finish the sentences about Julie.**

1 Julie *is* from New York in the USA.
2 She ... 20 years old.
3 She ... for a fashion company.
4 From Monday to Friday, she ... up at 6 o'clock, then she ... in the park.
5 She ... to work on the subway. She ... work at 8.
6 She ... home at 5 o'clock, she ... 'hello' to her friends, then she ... her supper.

Tips and tricks

Times and days:

on *Monday, Tuesday, Wednesday, ...*

in *the morning, the afternoon, the evening*

at *6 o'clock / the weekend*

R, P **E** **Florian has also written about himself online. Make sentences about him.**

A1.4

He's from ... *He's a ...* *At the weekend he ...*

Hey!

ABOUT ME My name's Florian Becker. I'm from Duisburg in Germany. I'm 17 and I'm a student at a vocational college.

MY WEEKEND I'm a student from Monday to Friday but at the weekend I'm me! On Saturday, I get up at midday. In the afternoon, I read magazines, I listen to music, or I go online. In the evening I meet my friends and we go to town. On Sunday morning I always go to the swimming pool, then I work out at a fitness club. In the afternoon I meet my friends again. In the evening, we often buy pizza and watch a movie at one of our homes.

P **F** **Now write about YOU.**

- What's your name?
- How old are you?
- Where are you from?
- Are you a student at a vocational college too?
- Write about your weekend.

Das *simple present*

Denk daran: *he / she / it* – das **s** muss mit!

I	work	get	go
he / she / it	work**s**	get**s**	go**es**
we you they	work work work	get get get	go go go

→ vocational college

6 What can you understand?

R, P **A Look at the pictures. Find …**

a waiter · a bus driver · a girl in a shoe shop · a hotel receptionist · a shop assistant · a mechanic · a man in a restaurant · a backpacker · a woman with a car

A

B

E

C

D

R
A1.5
B Listen to these five short conversations. Match the pictures and the conversations.

Conversation 1: *That's picture …*

R, P **C Listen again. What can you understand? Make sentences.**

1	The man in the restaurant wants …
2	The backpacker on the bus wants …
3	The woman with the mechanic has …
4	The man on the phone to the hotel wants …
5	The girl in the shoe shop wants …

A	to go to the youth hostel.
B	to know her shoe size in Germany.
C	to know about 'Gemüse'.
D	a problem with her car.
E	to book a room.

→ conversation → to want to (go) → on the phone

Hier und dort

Do you speak English?

Englisch hat sich zu einer echten Weltsprache entwickelt. Man begegnet ihr überall: in Liedern, mit native speakers auf einem Musikfest, auf Reisen, im Internet oder in der Arbeit mit ausländischen Kunden.

— In *Entry* hast du verschiedene Personen kennengelernt, die Englisch sprechen. Kennst du weitere Personen oder Situationen? Gib Beispiele.

— „Wenn Engländer oder Amerikaner in Deutschland Urlaub machen, sollten sie Deutsch können!" Findest du das auch?

7 Check-out

P **A Paul is a hotel receptionist at a hotel in London. Finish the text with the verbs on the right.**

Hey!
My name's Paul Everest and **(1)** *I'm* from England. I'm 21 years old and I **(2)** ... in London, England's capital city. I'm a hotel receptionist.

>>>> **My family** >>>>>>>>>>>>>>>>>>>>>>>>>>>>>>>>>>>>
My dad's name is John. He also **(3)** ... in a hotel. **(4)** ... a restaurant manager. My mum is a shop assistant. I **(5)** ... two younger brothers and one older sister. My two brothers **(6)** ... students at a vocational college in London. Gary (the youngest) **(7)** ... to be a mechanic and Jason a restaurant cook. My sister Jacqui **(8)** ... and she **(9)** ... two children. She **(10)** ... in the north of England.

>>>> **My job** >>
My hotel **(11)** ... the Heathrow Crown Hotel. There **(12)** ... about 250 rooms. There **(13)** ... also a restaurant. It is near London airport and we **(14)** ... always busy. From Monday to Friday I **(15)** ... work at 2 o'clock in the afternoon and I **(16)** ... at 10 o'clock in the evening. When I'm at work, I **(17)** ... the telephone, **(18)** ... rooms and welcome guests when they arrive at the hotel. I like my job very much. I **(19)** ... lots of interesting people from around the world.

>>>> **Free time!** >>>>>>>>>>>>>>>>>>>>>>>>>>>>>>>>>>>>
In my free time I jog, read, **(20)** ... to music and **(21)** ... the internet. I also **(22)** ... to a fitness club twice a week. But the best thing for me is my friends. At the weekends we usually **(23)** ... on the underground into the city. I **(24)** ... living in London. There **(25)** ... always so many interesting things to do.

answer
are (4 x)
book
finish
go
has
have
He's
I'm
is
is called
is married
listen
live
lives
love
meet
start
surf
travel
wants
works

P **B Write a short text about Paul's free time. Look at the last part of the text. Begin like this:**

In his free time Paul ...

P **C EXTRA Imagine you are one of Paul's brothers or his sister. Write about yourself.**

P **D Paul is speaking on the phone to a guest. Finish the conversation with words and phrases on the right.**

Paul **Guest**

Paul: Good morning. Heathrow Crown Hotel. Paul **(1)** ...

Guest: Hi. **(2)** ... a room for this evening, please.

Paul: Is that a single room or a double room?

Guest: A **(3)** ... , please.

Paul: I'm very sorry, sir. I **(4)** ... a single room this evening. But you can have a double room. It only costs another £10.

Guest: That's fine, thanks.

Paul: Can I take your **(5)** ... , please?

Guest: Yes, It's Kowalski, Scott Kowalski. I'm from Chicago, USA.

Paul: OK, Mr Kowalski. That's all booked.

Guest: (6) ...

Paul: **(7)** ... . (8) ...

Guest: Bye now.

Bye
don't have
I'd like to book
name
single
speaking
Thanks very much
You're welcome

R **E Write the times in words. There are three answers for one of the clocks!**

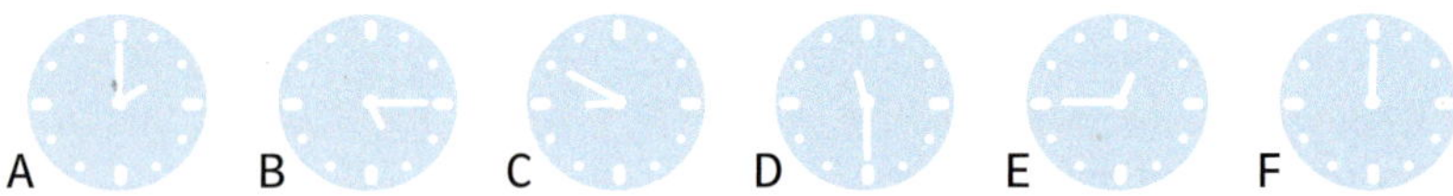

P **F Janine is an American college student. This is a picture of her with her friends. Finish the sentences. Use *my, your, his, her, our* and *their*.**

1 "Hi! *My* name's Janine. I'm a college student in the U.S."
2 Person A is one of Janine's friends. ... name is Bruce.
3 Next to Bruce is another friend. ... name is Julie-Ann.
4 The two people, C, are two more friends. ... names are Trudi and Don.
5 "Hi! We're the C people! ... names are Trudi and Don."
6 "And I'm person D. ... name's Max.
7 And you. What's ... name?

P **G TEST YOURSELF What can you do now? Find out! Choose the correct answer a, b or c.**

Question	a	b	c
1 My name's Charlotte. What's ... name? – I'm Christoph.	my	her	your
2 Where ... you from? – I'm from Germany.	are	is	am
3 This is my friend. ... name's Anja.	Their	Her	Our
4 My ... name is John.	brothers'	brothers	brother's
5 ... three rooms at the hostel for two people.	There's	There are	Is there
6 How many computers are there? – ... one.	There's	There are	Is there
7 ... smartphone? – Yes, and a laptop.	Have you	Does you have	Do you have
8 Mike has a PC but he ... have a laptop.	don't have	doesn't have	has not
9 Lots of people in my class ... a bike.	have	are have	is have
10 What time is it? – It's 3.30.	= half past four	= half past three	= half to four
11 What time is it now? – It's 6.45.	= a quarter past six	= a quarter before six	= a quarter to seven
12 Hi. My name's Mary-Lou and I ... in New York.	works	am work	work
13 At the weekend, Oliver ... up at midday.	is get	get	gets
14 Jack and his two friends often ... to the cinema at the weekend.	go	goes	are go
15 I'm from England. ... about you?	Where	What	From
16 Greg is from ...	australia.	Australien.	Australia.
17 Tony eats his lunch ... 1 o'clock.	on	at	in
18 I watch TV ... the evening.	on	at	in
19 White Horse Hotel. Nicole ...	speak.	speaking.	speaks.
20 Thanks very much. – You're ...	OK.	welcome.	goodbye.

CollegeNet
The International Network of Vocational Colleges

FIND A PARTNER >> search >> post a message

Here you can
- find partner colleges in more than 20 countries worldwide
- use the website as a platform to get to know students like you around the world
- organise projects between colleges
- organise international visits and exchanges

Country USA
College Kansas West Community College

Hey!
We are students in a class at KWCC (Kansas West Community College) in Kansas City, Kansas, USA. We would like to get to know students like us who are training for jobs at a college in another country. We would particularly like to hear from students from Europe. Interested? Leave us a message and we'll get back to you. Hoping to hear from you soon!

Unit 1
At college

2se2hk

1 CollegeNet

R, I, P **A Look at the picture on the left and answer these questions. Compare your answers with a partner, then tell the class.**

1 How many people are there in the picture?
There are …
2 How many boys are there and how many girls?
3 Where are they? At home? At college? In town? …?
4 What do you think? What country are they from?
We think …

Hier und dort

Sowohl in den USA als auch in Großbritannien und in einigen anderen englischsprachigen Ländern findet die Berufsbildung auf einem **college** statt, und die Lernenden sind **students**. In **Kickoff** benutzen wir durchgehend diese Wörter für dich und deine Schule.

R, P **B Read the web page and the message on the left.**

1 What city, country and college are the students from on page 20?
2 What is the name of the website where you can read their message?
3 Say something in your own words about the website (who is it for? what can you do on the site?)
4 What would these students 'particularly' like to do?
5 What must you do if you want to get to know these students better?

M **C Find the words and phrases in the students' message.**

„Wir werden uns wieder bei euch melden."

„Hallo!"

„Wir hoffen bald von euch zu hören!"

Am Ende von Unit 1 kann ich:

— über mich, meine Schule und meinen Kurs reden
— etwas von der beruflichen Erziehung in den USA erzählen
— eine Mitteilung ins Netz stellen.

→ community college (US) → to leave a message

2 Meet Clyde and Beth

R, P A1.6

A Read what Clyde says, then finish the sentences about him below.

Hi again. I'm Clyde. I'm 18 years old and I live in Kansas City, Kansas. I'm a student at KWCC, the Kansas West Community College. I'm on a business course, and when I finish the course, I want to work in a marketing company, maybe in Kansas City.
My course is full-time. I go to college five days a week from Monday to Friday. Most days, the lessons start at 8.30 in the morning and finish at around 2.30 in the afternoon. We get a lunch break from twelve to one. There are lots of sports clubs at KWCC and in the afternoons I usually play basketball or do athletics.
There are 20 people in my class. They're all great guys and I often hang out with them at the weekend.

1 Clyde *lives* in Kansas City.
2 He's on a business course and when he ... the course, he ... maybe to work in a marketing company.
3 Clyde ... to college five days a week.
4 Most days his lessons ... at 8.30. He ... a lunch break from twelve to one.
5 In the afternoons he usually ... basketball or he ... athletics.
6 He thinks the people in his class are OK. He often ... out with them at the weekend.

P **B What about YOU? Make sentences with the phrases on the right.**

"I'm ... years old."

"I'm a student at ..."

"I go to college ... days a week"

"My lessons ..."

"I live ..."

P **C Can you give the missing forms?**

The simple present → More please **A – C**

	want	live	go	finish
I	?	live	go	finish
he / she / it	wants	?	goes	finishes
we	want	live	?	finish
you	want	live	go	?
they	want	live	?	finish

Tips and tricks
Nicht vergessen:
he / she / it das *s* muss mit!

→ to be on a course → most days → to do athletics

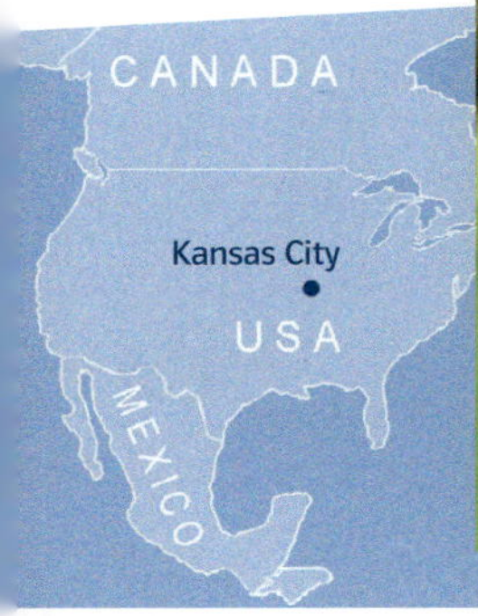

A1.7

D Now listen to Beth. Which is right? Note down a) or b).

1 Beth is a) 18 years old b) 19 years old.
2 She's in the a) first b) second year of her course.
3 She a) knows b) doesn't know what job she wants to have after college.
4 Her father a) works in an office b) is a truck driver.
5 She a) has b) doesn't have four brothers and sisters.
6 Kansas City a) is b) isn't in just one state.
7 The city has a) 500,000 b) 750,000 people.
8 Beth a) likes b) doesn't like Kansas City.

R, P **E What's the same and what's different for YOU? Copy and fill in the table below then make sentences.**

Beth is 18 but I'm not 18. I'm …

	Beth	Me
age	18	?
knows what job she wants?	?	?
family	?	?
likes where she lives?	?	?

P **F Can you give the missing forms?**

Das simple present: Verneinung		→ More please **D, E**
I	?	
he / she / it	?	live in California.
we / you / they	don't	

→ to finish sth → truck driver → kinda (US slang) = kind of

3 A brochure

R **A** **Read about Amber.**

Amber Johnson is a student at Oaklands High School in Kansas City. Almost all American teenagers go to high school and they leave when they're 18 years old. Amber is 18 now, so it's her last year at school. Next year she wants to go to KWCC. She wants to be a computer technician. Today, she has a brochure about the college. You can see a page from the brochure on page 25.

1 Where does she go to high school? How old is she?
2 What does she want to do next year?
3 What job does Amber want to have one day?

R **B** **Amber has lots of questions about the college and the courses there. Look at the brochure and find the answers for her.** → Skills 1

1 How big is the college and how many students are there?
2 How many courses does the college offer?
3 Can I train to be a computer technician?
4 How long do the courses last?
5 How much do the courses cost?
6 How can I contact the college?

P **C** **What about YOU?**

1 Where is your college? Does your college have a name?
2 How long does your course last?
3 How much does your course cost?

R **D** **Can you give the missing forms?**

Das simple present: Fragen			→ More please! F–H
Where	do	I	live?
	?	he / she / it	
	?	we / you / they	

→ to want to (do sth) → a brochure → to last (one year / two years) → to cost

A1.8

KANSAS WEST COMMUNITY COLLEGE

WHO DO YOU WANT TO BE?

With over 8,000 students, KWCC is one of the biggest community colleges in Kansas. Most students come to us after high school at 18, but the college is for everyone. Our oldest student at the moment is 75!

Because we are so big, we offer over 200 different courses. So whether you want to be a hairdresser or a secretary, a computer technician or a dancer, we can help you.

Courses at KWCC don't last 'a year' or 'two years'. You get 'credits' when you come to classes. When you have enough credits, you finish the course. So you can finish your course in one year, two years, or even longer if you want.

Courses cost between $1,000 and $5,000 dollars but you can get help with money if you need it. We have all the details – just come and talk to us.

COURSES AT KWCC

We offer courses in all these subject areas ...

> Art and Design
> Automotive Mechanics
> Business and Business Administration
> Computers and Information Technology
> Construction
> Health and Beauty
> Music and Media
> Retail Services
> Social Work and Child Care
> Sport
> Electronics

How to contact us:

Visit our website:
www.kwcc.edu

Email us at:
info@kwcc.edu

Call us on:
913 318-40 05 (toll free)

→ at the moment → enough → it costs ($1,000 dollars)

4 More please!

P △ **A Das simple present** → Grammar 1

Here are some more sentences about Clyde. Choose the correct forms of the verbs. Write out the correct sentences in full.

1 Clyde **lives** in the USA.
 a live b lives c livs
2 He … to work in a marketing company after college.
 a want b wants c wantes
3 He … to college every day from Monday to Friday.
 a go b gos c goes
4 He … a lunch break from 12 o'clock to 1 o'clock.
 a gets b get c getes
5 In the afternoons after his classes he often … basketball.
 a plays b play c playes
6 He also often … athletics.
 a do b dos c does
7 He … the other people in his class and often … out with them.
 a like / hangs b likes / hang c likes / hangs

I often hang out with my friends at the weekend.

P △ **B Das simple present** → Grammar 1

Finish these sentences about YOU in your own words.

1 Hi! My name … (to be) … (your name).
2 I … (to live) in … (town) in Germany and I … (to be) … (number) years old.
3 I … (to go) to a vocational college in … (town). It … (to be) called … (name of college).
4 My lessons usually … (to start) at … (time) and they normally … (to finish) at … (time).
5 There … (to be) … (number) people in my class today.
6 When I'm not at college, I often … (to go to town? to play … ? to do …? to hang out with …? …?)

P ▲ **C Das simple present** → Grammar 1

Finish the text about Ray with the correct forms of the verbs on the right. You can use some of the verbs more than once. Then imagine you are Ray. Write a short text about yourself.

Ray (1) is a student at KWCC. He (2) … on a business course at the college and when he (3) … the course he (4) … to travel and to work in Europe – maybe in Germany. Ray's family came from Germany and he (5) … an uncle there. His uncle (6) … in Cologne. Ray (7) … to college five days a week. His lessons normally (8) … at 8.30 and they (9) … at 2.30. KWCC (10) … its own radio station and in the afternoons Ray often (11) … in the studio: he is good with technical things. Ray really (12) … the other people in his class. He (13) … that they are friendly and open. Ray and the other students often (14) … together at the weekend. They (15) … to the mall in the city centre or, in the summer, to the park.

to be
to finish
to go
to hang out
to have
to like
to live
to start
to think
to want
to work

D Das simple present: Verneinung → Grammar 1

All the information about Beth below is false! Correct the information like this:

No! Beth doesn't live in New York! She lives in …

Beth > lives in New York.
> She is 99 years old.
> She hates her city.
> She has 14 brothers.
> She wants to be an astronaut.

EXTRA Write five sentences about yourself. Make the sentences negative. Like this:

I don't live in the USA. I'm not … I …

E Das simple present: Verneinung → Grammar 1

For each sentence below, write a sentence that is negative. Like this:

I have brothers and sisters. *I don't have brothers and sisters.*

1 Beth lives in California.
2 She likes computer games.
3 She has blond hair.
4 She's 27 years old.
5 I'm a student at a college in China.
6 I go to college seven days a week.
7 I'm extremely rich and I have four cars and a private plane.
8 There are 100 people in my class.
9 We learn German in our English lessons.
10 You come from the planet Delta III.
11 They use their phones in their lessons.
12 The students get a lunch break.

Tips and tricks

Denk daran!
Beth lives in the USA.
*She doesn't **live** in Germany.*
*She doesn't ~~**lives**~~ in Germany.*

F Das simple present: Fragen *(to be)* → Grammar 1

You are talking to Amber. Make questions for her with the verb *to be*.

1 Where / you / from?
Where are you from?
2 What class / you / in / at high school?
3 How big / your school?
4 How old / you?
5 When / you / 18?
6 When / your birthday?
7 How far / KWCC / from your home?
8 What / your hobbies?
9 you / a sporty person?

She comes from the planet Delta III.

P △ **G Das simple present: Fragen (Hauptverben)** → Grammar 1

Give the missing words to make the questions.

1 Where *does* Amber *live* (live)?
2 What … she … (want) to do next year?
3 Why … Americans … (go) to a community college?
4 How long … the courses there … (last)?
5 How much … they … (cost)?
6 Where … you … (live)?
7 Where … you … (go) to college?
8 When … your lessons … (start) and when … they … (finish)?
9 What … you … (want) to do after college?
10 Why … you … (want) to have that job?

Tips and tricks
Denke daran!
He lives in the USA.
*Where does he **live**?*
Where does he ~~lives~~?

P ▲ **H Das simple present: Fragen** → Grammar 1

You are talking to an American community college student. Here are his answers to your questions – but what were your questions? Write them down.

1 My name is Romano.
What's your name?
2 I live in Chicago, Illinois.
3 I'm 18 years old.
4 I go to college in Chicago.
5 I want to be an electrician when I finish my course.
6 I want to be an electrician because I think it's an interesting job – and my dad is an electrician.
7 There are around 5,000 students at my college.
8 I have lessons five days a week.
9 I go to college by bus.
10 It (= my course) costs $1,500.
11 Yes, I have a part-time job – I work in a fast food restaurant.
12 Yeah, I think my college is great. The teachers are all good and the course is very practical.

P ▲ **I Key words**

Look at the words at the bottom of pages 21 – 25. Choose the best words to finish the sentences below.

1 – How much do the courses …?
– It depends. The most expensive are around $5,000.
2 A … … is a place where people train for jobs. In the States, these are called … ….
3 I want to be a computer technician when I finish college. I'm on an IT … at college.
4 I'm not at college. … … … I'm in my room.
5 If you want to contact us, you can leave a … on the CollegeNet website.
6 Kansas City is … strange – it's in two states.
7 You can find out more about the college if you read this … – it gives you all the information you need.

5 Now you

P, I **A Look back at the message from the students at KWCC on page 20. You would like to get to know them. Post a message on the website.**

1 In groups, write a message back.
2 Compare messages then write one as a class that you can post. Ask a student to write it on the board.

> Hey!
> We saw your message on the CollegeNet noticeboard.
> We are ...

TIP
The text of messages, letters and emails in English always begins with a CAPITAL letter! You can start a message like this:
Dear (name), Hi, Hey, Hello

You can finish like this:
Looking forward to hearing from you (soon).
Hoping you get back to us (soon).

P, I **B It is two months since you first saw the message from the KWCC students and now you regularly write to them in your English lessons. Work in small groups. Choose one of the topics on the right and write a text. Put your texts up around the classroom so that students can walk round and read them (a 'gallery walk').**
→ Skills 16

your town
your college
Germany
your course
your job plans
the sport(s) that you like

V1

Video Lounge A stopover in New York

Three British students, Maya, Greg and Josh, win a film competition. Their prize is a holiday in Hollywood. In this video, the three arrive in America and have a stopover in New York before they fly to Los Angeles.

P, P, I **Watch the video and answer the questions. Compare your answers with a partner, then report to the class.**

1 How do the students travel from the airport to their hotel in New York City?
2 What three famous sights do they see on the way?
3 Who is Amy?
4 What mistake with American English does the British student Greg make?
5 What does Greg bet his friends that he can do?
6 What must his friends do at the end of the video? Why?

JOB PROFILE fitness trainer

What does a fitness trainer do?
A fitness trainer (or personal trainer) helps people with exercises and exercise machines. (S)he also often talks to people about their diets and a healthy lifestyle.

Where does a fitness trainer work?
A fitness trainer usually works inside in a fitness club or a sports centre.

When does a fitness trainer work?
The hours of work for a fitness trainer can be long. Fitness clubs are often open in the evenings and at weekends.

Fitness trainers usually like ...
sport, keeping fit, helping people, working with people.

A1.9

Unit 2
People and jobs

9563bz

1 A careers website

P, I **A Work in a small group. Write down in English as many jobs as you can in five minutes, then make a list in class.**

P, I **B Look at the picture on the left. The student in the picture is Daniel and he's from Australia. He wants to find out about different jobs. In your group again, answer the questions below, then report to the class.**

1 What exactly is Daniel doing at the moment? For example, is he sitting in a classroom? using a laptop? listening to music?
2 Why is he doing this?
3 And YOU. What are you doing right now?

R **C Look at the job profile on the left from a careers website. True or false?** → More please! A – B

1 A fitness trainer usually works outside – for example, at a sports stadium.
2 A fitness trainer doesn't usually like sport.
3 A fitness trainer often works with people.
4 Fitness clubs are never open at the weekends.
5 A fitness trainer often talks to people about what they eat and how they live.

P, I **D Talk in class**

1 Where do you want to work one day? Do you want to work inside (for example, in an office) or outside?
2 Are you a friendly person? Do you want to work with people or to help people?

→ hours of work → usually → often → inside → outside

Tips and tricks

*He **usually works** in a fitness club. The club **is often** open on Saturdays.*

Adverbien wie *usually, often, always, never* usw. stehen direkt **vor** einem Hauptverb, aber **nach** *to be.*

Am Ende von Unit 2 kann ich:

— mehrere Berufe beschreiben,
— sagen, warum man gewisse Jobs vorzieht,
— sagen, was Leute oft oder gewöhnlich machen und was sie gerade im Moment machen.

2 Which job?

R, P **A Read what these four people say and the job profiles below and on page 33. What do you think? Which job is best for each person? Why?**

I think the best job for person A is a … because (s)he …
Person B wants to … / likes … and so I think the best job for her / him is a …

A B C D

A
I want to work with my hands. I really like mechanical things – my hobby is go-karting.

B
I don't want to work inside. I hate offices! I like flowers and plants.

C
I love fashion and beauty. I want to work with my hands. And I'm a really friendly person. I want to meet lots of people in my job.

D
I have five small brothers and sisters. I want to work in a team and to help kids.

A 1.10

JOB PROFILE GARDENER

What does a gardener do?
A gardener looks after flowers and plants, cuts grass etc.

Where does a gardener work?
Gardeners usually work outside in gardens or parks. They sometimes also work in garden centres.

When does a gardener work?
A gardener normally works five days a week but the hours can be longer in the summer.

Gardeners usually like:
nature, being outside.

JOB PROFILE MECHANIC

What does a mechanic do?
A mechanic repairs and services cars and other vehicles.

Where does a mechanic work?
Mechanics usually work in a workshop.

When does a mechanic work?
Workshops are normally open five days a week from around 7.30 a.m. to around 6 p.m.

Mechanics usually like:
mechanical things, working with their hands, working in a team.

→ each → normally

A

B

C

D

P **B** **Look at the four pictures. What are the people's jobs? What are they doing at the moment in the pictures? Use the verbs on the right.**

Person A is a … Right now he's …

work play cut sit talk wash repair

P **C** **Can you give the missing forms?**

Das present continuous		→ More please C – E
I	am	working.
he / she / it	?	sitting.
we / you / they	?	playing.

JOB PROFILE NURSERY ASSISTANT

What does a nursery assistant do?
A nursery assistant looks after young children 2–5 years old. (S)he plays with children, reads stories, helps the smaller children etc.

Where does a nursery assistant work?
Nursery assistants work in private or state nurseries.

When does a nursery assistant work?
Most nurseries are open five days a week from around 7.30 a.m. to around 5.00 or 6.00 p.m.

Nursery assistants usually like:
children, working in a team, meeting and helping people.

JOB PROFILE HAIRDRESSER

What does a hairdresser do?
A hairdresser cuts men's and women's hair.

Where does a hairdresser work?
A hairdresser usually works in a salon with other hairdressers.

When does a hairdresser work?
Salons are usually open five or six days a week from around 9 a.m. to around 5 p.m.

Hairdressers usually like:
fashion and beauty, meeting people, working in a team, working with their hands.

→ to look after → around (7.30 a.m.) → open from … to …

3 An interview in Australia

R
A 1.11

A **A reporter from ABC Radio in Australia is in the small town of Turkey Creek today. She's interviewing Pete Collins. Pete has six jobs. What are they? Listen and put the pictures 1–6 below in the right order.**

1 2 3 4 5 6

→ hunter → to hunt → customer

P **B Make sentences about Pete and his jobs. Use the phrases below. You can listen to the interview again if you need to.**

In the mornings Pete / he ...

When?	What?	Where?
In the mornings In the afternoons In the evenings Sometimes	he cuts hair he works as a barman he delivers letters and packages he repairs cars he hunts crocodiles he serves customers	in his workshop. everywhere in Turkey Creek. in his bar. in the river. in his shop. in his hairdressing 'salon'.

P, I **C Make questions about Pete's day. Ask another student in your class.**

What does Pete do in the mornings? – In the mornings he ...
Then he ...
When does he cut hair? – He cuts hair ...
Where does he serve customers? – He serves customers ...

R A 1.12 **D Listen to these six short conversations. Which job is Pete doing at the moment? What's he doing in each conversation?**

Pete is a ... at the moment. He's ...

P, I **E Work with a partner. Ask questions about the pictures on page 34.**

What's Pete doing in this picture?
– He's delivering letters and packages.

P, I **F Talk about Turkey Creek and Pete.** → More please! F – H

1 Where is Turkey Creek? In northern / southern / eastern / western Australia? Is it a big or a small town?
2 What do you think? Does Pete have a nice life? Why (not)?

→ northern → southern → eastern → western

Hier und dort

Einige Unterschiede zwischen Deutschland und Australien:

- **Größe:**
  Deutschland 357 000 km^2,
  Australien 7,7 Millionen km^2.
- **Bevölkerung:**
  Deutschland 82 Millionen,
  Australien 20 Millionen.
- **Temperatur im Dezember:**
  Deutschland 5 °C,
  Australien 30 °C.

4 More please!

P ▲ **A Das simple present mit Adverbien** → Grammar 1

Decide where the adverb belongs – a) or b). Then write out the sentence in full with the adverb(s) in the correct place.

Example:
(usually) I a) ... come b) ... to college by bike. (Answer: a)
I usually come to college by bike.

1 (often) Hairdressers a) ... work b) ... in a salon.
2 (always) In England, shops a) ... are b) ... open on Sundays.
3 (never) Mike is a nursery assistant. He a) ... works b) ... on Sundays.
4 (always / often) Gardeners in big parks a) ... are b) ... busy but they a) ... are b) ... particularly busy in the summer.
5 (usually / sometimes) Deb is a mechanic. She a) ... repairs b) ... cars but she a) ... repairs b) ... motor bikes, too.

P, R ▲ **B Das simple present mit Adverbien** → Grammar 1

Write these sentences again and put in the best adverbs on the right. Put the adverbs in the correct place in the sentences. More than one adverb is sometimes correct.

1 Gardeners are people who like plants and flowers.
Gardeners are normally people who like plants and flowers.
2 Kim is a nursery assistant. She does some things every day – for example, in the afternoons, she reads her children a story.
3 Car workshops are open on Sundays.
4 When the weather is nice, the park in my town is full of people.
5 Hairdressers work in a salon but they go to people's homes, too, if the people are old or ill.
6 Fitness trainers are people who like sport and helping people. They work in a fitness club but they talk to people about diets and lifestyles, too.

sometimes
often
never
usually / normally
(almost) always

P ▲ **C Das present continuous *(to be)*** → Grammar 2

Finish the sentences with the correct forms of *to be*. Use full forms *(am, is, are)*. Then choose three sentences and write them again with the short forms *('m, 's, 're)*.

1 Alison is a hairdresser. At the moment, she ... washing a man's hair.
2 The children are at the nursery. Right now, they ... playing.
3 Three gardeners ... working in the park today.
4 Jake is a secretary. He ... talking on the phone at the moment. His girlfriend Emma is at work, too. She's a fitness trainer. She ... helping a woman with an exercise machine.
5 What ... you doing at the moment? I ... learning English.

What are the kids doing at the moment?
It's 'quiet hour'. They're sleeping.

P, R ▲

D Das present continuous (*-ing* forms) ⟶ Grammar 2

Copy and complete the table with the *-ing* forms of the verbs. Then use the forms to complete the sentences. Use each form only once.

to work	working	to cut	?
to do	?	to sit	?
to listen	?	to dance	?
to play	?	to use	?

1 James is a mechanic. What's he *doing* right now? He's ... in the workshop and he's ... to music on his radio.
2 The nursery assistant is ... the guitar and the children are ... .
4 Lily is ... a man's hair at the moment. The man is ... in a chair.
5 Are you ... a laptop at the moment?

P ▲

E Das present continuous ⟶ Grammar 2

Finish the sentences with the *present continuous* forms of the verbs. You can use the short forms of *to be* when possible. Be careful with the spellings of the *–ing* forms!

1 Daniel *is sitting* (sit) on a beach at the moment. He ... (use) a laptop. He ... (look at) a careers website.
2 The fitness trainer ... (help) two men with an exercise. The men ... (lift) some weights.
3 James likes mechanical things. Right now, he ... (drive) a go-kart.
4 There are three hairdressers in the salon today. Two ... (cut) people's hair. One ... (wash) someone's hair.
5 The children are at the nursery at the moment. Their teacher ... (play) the guitar. The children ... (listen) and they ... (dance).
6 I ... (go) to college at the moment. I ... (sit) in a bus and I ... (do) my homework.

P ▲

F Simple present oder present continuous? ⟶ Grammar 2

Finish the sentences about Pete with the right forms of the verbs. In one sentence (a or b) the verb is in the *simple present*, in the other it is in the *present continuous*.

1 (to deliver) a Pete *delivers* letters every morning.
b It's 9 a.m. and he *'s delivering* letters at the moment.
2 (to work) a Pete ... in his bar at the moment.
b He always ... in his bar in the evenings.
3 (to cut) a In the afternoons, Pete ... hair.
b He ... someone's hair right now.
4 (to hunt) a Pete sometimes ... crocodiles (well, he says so!)
b He ... a crocodile right now.
5 (to serve) a Pete ... a customer in his shop at the moment.
b He ... customers there every day, usually in the mornings.
6 (do / repair) a What ... (Pete) at the moment? He ... a car.
b He always ... people's cars in Turkey Creek.

So läuft's besser

Vokabellernen ist immer etwas schmerzhaft – aber das muss sein, um in der Sprache weiterzukommen. Zwei Tipps:

— Schreibe neue Vokabeln immer in ein Vokabelheft und wiederhole sie regelmäßig.
— Formuliere mit den neuen Wörtern ganze Sätze oder Redewendungen. Auf diese Weise kannst du erkennen wie sie verwendet werden und in Verbindung mit welchen Worten sie häufig auftauchen.

P, R ▲ **G Simple present oder present continuous?** → Grammar 2

Your class is in England and today you are visiting the kitchen of a famous restaurant. One of the chefs there is showing you round. Finish what he says. Use the *simple present* or the *present continuous*. Use your dictionary if there are words that you don't know.

Hi and welcome to our kitchen. I work here as a chef. OK, what is a typical day for us?

Well, we usually (1) *start* (start) work at 8 o'clock in the morning. We (2) ... (serve) two meals every day – lunch and dinner. Right now, at 11 o'clock, we (3) ... (prepare) lunch. On the menu today we have a special lamb with garlic sauce, so at the moment, some of my colleagues over there (4) ... (cook) the meat and some (5) ... (cut up) vegetables. And this is Marie. She (6) ... (make) the sauce. OK, we normally (7) ... (finish) serving lunch at about 2.30, and in the afternoons we are free. We (8) ... (come) back to work again at 4.30 to get ready for dinner in the evening. We finally (9) ... (finish) for the day at about midnight. Chefs (10) ... (work) very hard!

P △ **H Describing pictures.** → Grammar 2

Finish the text about Pete. Use the *present continuous* to say what Pete is doing and what is happening in the scene.

In this picture, you can see Pete, the Australian man with six jobs. Pete is at the airport at the moment, he is working as a postman. He (1) *is standing* (stand) on the right. He (2) ... (hold) his bike and he (3) ... (wear) cycling shorts. In the foreground, there is a post bag with lots of letters. In the background there is a plane. It (4) ... (take off). It is a post plane.

▲ **EXTRA Look at page 34 of your book. Describe one of the other pictures of Pete. Say where Pete is, his job right now, what you can see and where, and what the people in the picture are doing, wearing etc. Use your dictionary to look up words you don't know.**

5 Now you

P, I **A This questionnaire is from the CollegeNet website. Work in groups and answer the questions for you. Read your answers to the class at the end.**

Hello all college students! We'd like to have your ideas about jobs! Please write to us and give us your answers to these questions.

1 What's your name and where do you live?
2 Where do you go to college and what course are you on?
3 What things do you want in a job? (Do you want to work with your hands, to meet lots of people, ... ?)
4 What do you want to do after college? What job do you (maybe) want to have?

Just go to the CollegeNet website and post your answers on the Jobs Questionnaire page www.collegenet.com/jobsquestionnaire

P, I **B Work in small groups again. Think of a job that you all know about – maybe one that you would like to have one day. Write a 'job profile'. Use the job profiles on pages 32–33 as models. Organise a 'gallery walk' or put up your profiles in the classroom.** → Skills 16

JOB PROFILE POSTMAN

What does a postman do?
A postman or postwoman delivers letters, packages etc.
Where does a postman work?
...

V2

Video Lounge Working as a receptionist

R, P

Sally is a receptionist in a company in England. Watch the video and finish the sentences.

1 The visitors want to see Diane Kennedy at ... (time)
2 Sally asks the visitors for their ...
3 Then she uses the phone to call ...
4 The visitors must complete a ...
5 Then Sally gives them ...

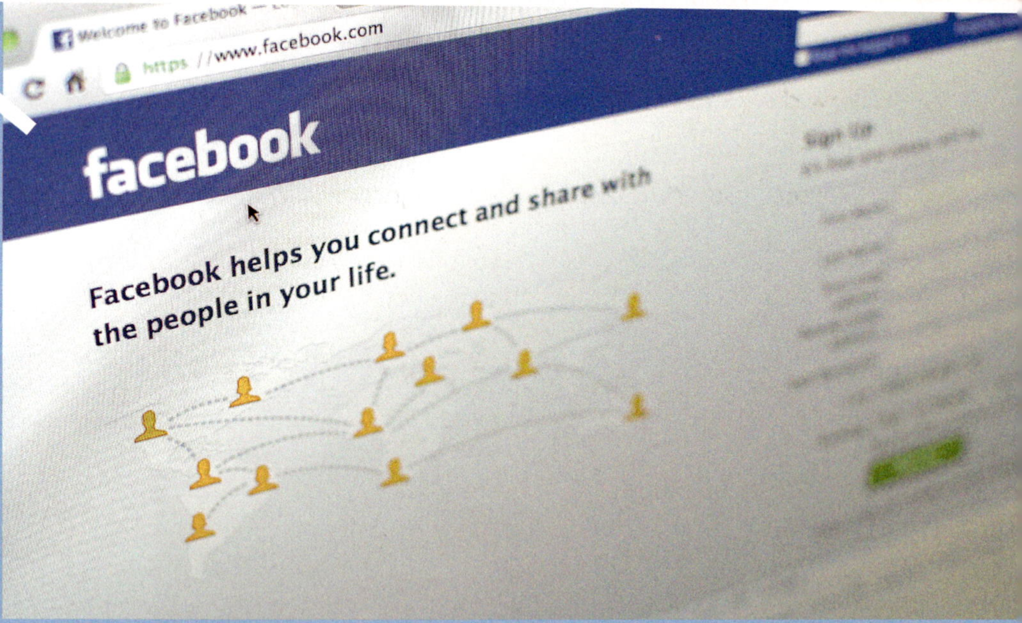

Unit 3
Products and services

1 Bringing the world together

R, P
A1.13

A Do you know the name of the man in the picture on the left? Read the text below for some clues!

In 2004, he was 23 years old and a student at Harvard University in the USA. He liked computers and, with four friends, he started a website. It was a site where students at Harvard could 'meet', get help with their university work, and talk about the things and the people they liked. He called it 'The Facebook'. Soon, students at other universities joined, then American high school students – and finally people worldwide. In October 2012, 'Facebook' got its one billionth user (1 billion = one thousand million). In Britain today, over half the population is on Facebook. In the USA it is 45 percent of the population. It is the world's biggest social networking service.

P, I

B Make a 'cheat sheet' for the text above. Give a short talk to the class. → Skills 15

P, I

C What about YOU? Write answers to these questions. Compare with a partner, then talk in class.

1 Facebook is a social networking site. Can you name other sites like it?
2 Are you on a social networking site? If 'yes', which one? When did you join? What do you do there?
Yes, I'm on …
I follow …
I joined in … / last year / … ago.
I usually / often …
3 If 'no', why not? Give two reasons.
I'm not …
First, I think …
Another reason is that …

Am Ende von Unit 3 kann ich:

— über die Vergangenheit sprechen und schreiben,
— über einige bekannte Produkte und Dienstleistungen sprechen und schreiben.

→ product / service → to join sth

2 Trainers then and now

R A **Read this magazine article about the history of trainers.**

A 1.14

1 When did sports shoes first start?
2 What famous company started in 1924? (Where?)
3 What important thing for trainers happened in the 1950s?

The history of trainers

Plimsolls and sneakers

The first sports shoes started over 100 years ago. They were called 'plimsolls'. They had a flat rubber sole and a canvas top and they were very simple – the left foot and the right foot were the same! In 1917, the U.S. Rubber Company made the first really comfortable plimsolls. They called them Keds. Soon, people called the new shoes 'sneakers'. 'To sneak' means 'to walk quietly'.

Sports shoes from Germany

In 1924, two German brothers started a sports shoe company in a small village in Germany. Their shoes had spikes and they were for athletes. The two bothers' names were Adi and Rudolf Dassler. Adi called the company, yes, Adidas. Athletes used Adidas shoes in lots of Olympic Games and they were soon famous. They were the best sports shoes in the world.

Trainers and fashion

In the 1930s and 40s people wore trainers for sports like athletics and basketball. Then in the 1950s a famous, young American actor, James Dean, wore trainers, jeans and a T-shirt in a movie. Trainers were now fashionable – and cheap. Soon, young people everywhere wore trainers (and jeans) too.

Hi-tech trainers

In the 1960s and 70s, companies started making hi-tech trainers. The Nike company started in the USA in 1968. Nike, Adidas and other companies made trainers with air in the soles of their shoes. Today, everyone loves trainers. In the USA, people buy around 350 million pairs every year!

→ history →comfortable →fashionable

R **B** **Find the missing verbs in the article.**

1 The first sports shoes	*started*	over 100 years ago.
2 They were called 'plimsolls' and they	?	very simple.
3 Plimsolls	?	a flat rubber sole and a canvas top.
4 The U.S. Rubber Company	?	the first comfortable plimsolls in 1917.
5 The company	?	the trainers Keds.
6 But soon people everywhere	?	them 'sneakers'.
7 In 1924, Adi and Rudolf Dassler	?	Adidas.
8 Adidas trainers	?	spikes.
9 They	?	for athletes.
10 Lots of athletes	?	Adidas trainers in the Olympic Games.
11 Soon Adidas sports shoes	?	famous.
12 In the 1950s, James Dean	?	trainers and jeans in a movie.
13 After his movie, trainers	?	fashionable – and cheap!
14 Companies like Nike	?	making hi-tech trainers in the 60s and 70s.
15 These hi-tech trainers	?	air in the soles.

P **C** **Look at the verbs in exercise B. Which verbs are 'regular'? Which are 'irregular'? Make two lists.**

P **D** **Make questions and answers about trainers.**

1 when / first sports shoes / start
*When **did** the first sports shoes **start**? – They **started** over 100 years ago.*
2 when / the U.S. Rubber Company / make the first comfortable plimsolls
3 what / people / call / Keds
4 when / Adi and Rudolf Dassler / start / Adidas
5 where / athletes / use / Adidas shoes / in the 1920s and 30s
6 why / people / wear / trainers / in the 1930s and 40s

Tips and tricks
*Adidas started **in** 1924.*
*They wore trainers **in** the 1930s.*
*The first sports shoes started 100 years **ago*** (= vor 100 Jahren).

P, I **E** **Ask the class more questions with *when*, *where* or *why*.**

P **F** **Can you give the missing forms?**

Das simple past → More please **A – D**

	regular	irregular	Fragen
	to start	to make	When ? it start? What ? he wear in the movie?
I	started	?	

→ athlete (athletics) → company → ago

3 The history of a company

R
A1.15

A Listen to Tanja Kugler and put the pictures 1–8 below in the right order.

Tanja Kugler works for the Coca-Cola® company in Germany. She works in the Public Relations (PR) department and today she's talking to some visitors to the company. Tanja is talking about the company's history.

Coca-Cola

1

The original logo
designed by Frank Robinson

5

2

3

Asa Candler and
Dr John S. Pemberton

4

Coca-Cola in bottles

8

6

Coca-Cola in China

7

Coca-Cola in cans

→ department (of a company) → pharmacist/pharmacy → assistant

Coca-Cola trucks from 1934 and the 1980s

R **B** **Listen again. True or false? Note down T or F.**

A 1.15

1 Dr John Pemberton made the first Coca-Cola in Atlanta, Georgia, in 1886.
2 His assistant invented the name Coca-Cola.
3 Dr Pemberton sold his business to a businessman in Atlanta called Frank Robinson.
4 The famous Coca-Cola bottle started in 1960.
5 The company produced the first Coca-Cola in Germany in Frankfurt.
6 The Coca-Cola company invented Fanta in Germany in 1940.
7 The first Coca-Cola in cans was in 1982.
8 Today, people drink Coca-Cola in over 20 countries around the world.

P **C** **All the sentences below are wrong! Can you correct them?**

1 Dr Pemberton invented the name Coca-Cola. (Frank Robinson)
*Wrong! Dr Pemberton **didn't invent** the name. His assistant Frank Robinson **invented** the name.*
2 At first, people bought Coca-Cola in bottles. (in glasses)
3 The Coca-Cola company produced the first Coca-Cola in Germany in 1999. (1929)
4 The company invented Fanta in the USA. (Germany)
5 The company sold the first Diet Coke in 2002. (1982)

P, I **D** **And YOU? Think of the time when you were six years old. Say three things you didn't do or didn't have then.**

When I was six, I didn't speak English. I didn't have …

P **E** **Can you give the missing forms?**

Das simple past: Verneinungen → More please **E – F**

I		start
he / she / it		make
we	?	invent
you		sell
they		drink

→ to invent → can (of a drink) → at first

So läuft's besser

Es gibt einige Verben, die in der Vergangenheitsform nicht auf *-ed* wie *I walk**ed*** enden: die unregelmäßigen Verben. Sie zu lernen ist einfach, wenn du dir jeden Tag ein Verb vornimmst und die Verben in Gruppen lernst wie z. B. *drink – dr**a**nk – dr**u**nk* und *sing – s**a**ng – s**u**ng*. Vgl. hierzu die Auflistung im Klappumschlag.

4 More please!

P △ **A Das simple past** → Grammar 3

Finish the sentences with the *simple past* forms of the verbs. Use the irregular verb page at the back of your book to find the verbs that are irregular.

1 (make) The US Rubber Company *made* the first comfortable plimsolls in 1917.
2 (give) They ... the plimsolls the name Keds.
3 (like) People ... them very much.
4 (wear / call) When people ... the Keds they walked very quietly – so they ... them 'sneakers'.
5 (live / come) Adi and his brother Rudolf Dassler ... in Germany. They ... from a small village there.
6 (win) Athletes often ... their races because of their Adidas shoes.
7 (be) James Dean ... an American movie star in the 1950s.
8 (see / want) When young people in the 1950s ... James Dean's movies, they ... trainers (and jeans), too.
9 (start) In the 60s and 70s, companies in Europe and America ... making hi-tech trainers.
10 (buy) Now you can see trainers everywhere. Last year, Americans ... 350 million pairs.

Now everyone loves trainers

P ▲ **B Das simple past** → Grammar 3

Test your irregular verbs! Complete the sentences with the *simple past* forms of the irregular verbs below, then check your answers with the irregular verb page at the back of your book.

1 (make) The US Rubber Company *made* the first comfortable plimsolls in 1917.
2 (be / have) They ... extremely simple – they ... just a flat rubber sole and a canvas top.
3 (feel) But they ... really comfortable and people liked them.
4 (can / give) You ... walk very quietly in them, so people ... them the name 'sneakers'.
5 (put) The Dassler brothers ... spikes on their sports shoes in the 1920s.
6 (hear / run) Many famous athletes ... about Adidas shoes and they often ... in them in their races.
7 (go) Lots of people ... to the cinema regularly in the 1950s.
8 (know) They ... the famous actors well and one of these was a young American star called James Dean.
9 (wear / think) He often ... trainers and jeans, and the young audiences ... he was really cool.
10 (buy / become) So they ... these items, too. Suddenly, trainers ... fashionable.
11 (find / sell) In the 60s and 70s, companies like Nike ... new ways to make trainers more hi-tech and they ... many millions of the new trainers.

P **C Das simple past (Fragen)** → Grammar 3

Below there are some facts about trainers. Complete the questions.

1 Trainers started in the USA.
Where *did* trainers *start*?
2 The American company made the first plimsolls in 1917.
When ... the American company ... the first plimsolls?
3 People called Keds 'sneakers' because you could walk quietly in them.
Why ... people ... Keds 'sneakers'?
4 The Dassler brothers came from a small village in Germany.
Where ... the Dassler brothers ... from?
5 Their shoes became famous because many athletes used them in the Olympic Games.
Why ...?
6 Young people saw a famous actor with trainers in the 1950s.
When ...
7 The Nike company started making hi-tech trainers in the 1960s and 70s.
When ...?
8 Americans bought 350 million trainers last year.
How many ...?

P **D Das simple past (Fragen)** → Grammar 3

Here are some facts about trainers. Write questions so that the facts are the answers.

1 Trainers started in the USA.
Where did trainers start?
2 They (the U.S. Rubber Company) started making plimsolls in 1917.
3 The company called them 'Keds'.
4 But ordinary people called them 'sneakers'.
5 Adidas sports shoes had spikes on their soles.
6 Athletes often won their races because they wore the new Adidas shoes.
7 Young people in the 1950s began wearing trainers because a famous actor wore them in his movies.
8 Jeans also became popular at that time because of the same actor.
9 The Nike Company started in 1968.
10 Last year, Americans bought around 350 million pairs of trainers.

P
▲ **E Das simple past (Verneinung)** → Grammar 3

Jake and Jenny are both students at the same college in England but yesterday they did very different things. Read about Jake, then finish the sentences about Jenny.

1 Jake got up at 7.30. Jenny *didn't get up* at 7.30, she *got up* at 8.00.
2 Jake had coffee and toast for breakfast. Jenny ... coffee and toast, she ... muesli and orange juice.
3 Jake came to college by bus. Jenny ... to college on the bus, she ... by bike.
4 Jake had his first lesson at 9.00. Jenny ... her first lesson then, she had it at 10.30.
5 Jake ate a sandwich for lunch. Jenny ... a sandwich, she ... an apple.
6 Jake finished his lessons at 3.30 yesterday. Jenny ... finish at 3.30, she ... at 5.30.
7 In the evening, Jake went on Facebook. Jenny ... on Facebook, she ... (watch) a DVD.
8 Jake sent texts to his friends, too. Jenny ... texts to her friends – she ... (phone) them.

P
▲ **F Das simple past (Verneinung)** → Grammar 3

Do exercise E above, then write about three more things that Jake and Jenny did differently yesterday. Write sentences like those in exercise E. Here are some ideas to get you started.

do a test in an English lesson · go to the gym after college · ...

M
▲ **G Key words**

Look at the words at the bottom of pages 41–45. Use them to translate the sentences below into English.

1 Facebook und Twitter sind Soziale Netzwerke im Internet.
2 Wann bist Du Facebook beigetreten?
3 Die Firma hat eine interessante Geschichte.
4 Chrissy kleidet sich sehr modisch.
5 Mein Bruder arbeitet in der Marketingabteilung einer großen Berliner Firma.
6 Ein Apotheker arbeitet in einer Apotheke.
7 Ich hätte gerne eine Dose Cola.
8 Steven Sasson erfand die Digitalkamera *(digital camera)* 1975.

5 Now you

R, P, I **A The text below is about the invention of mobile phones – but some information is missing. Work with a partner.**

Partner A: Please look at page 81 now.
Partner B: Answer your partner's questions. Then ask your questions to find the missing facts in this article.

This man's name is Dr Martin Cooper. He invented the modern mobile phone. He tested it for the first time on 3 April (1) ... (year). On that day, he made the first phone call in (2) ... (city). Ten years later, the Motorola company produced the first commercial mobile phones – mobile phones that everyone could buy. They (3) ... (had? didn't have?) text messaging or cameras. They weighed over 1 kilogram! And in today's money they cost around (4) $ ... !

M **B Your friend wants to know about the products and services in this unit but doesn't speak English. Choose one text and give your friend the most important information in German.**

V3

Video Lounge Making movies

R **Watch the video. True (T) or false (F)?**

1 In the first scene, the three students are making a movie.
2 It is a science-fiction movie.
3 Josh shoots Greg in the leg.
4 The blood in the packet is not real blood.
5 In film studios, they can make a hole in clothes with a remote control.
6 Greg must carry a transmitter in his pocket.
7 The director can't stay because he is making a movie next door.
8 Unfortunately, the three students can't watch him at work in the studio.
9 Before they leave, Maya has to give back the shoes she wore in the movie.

1

2

3

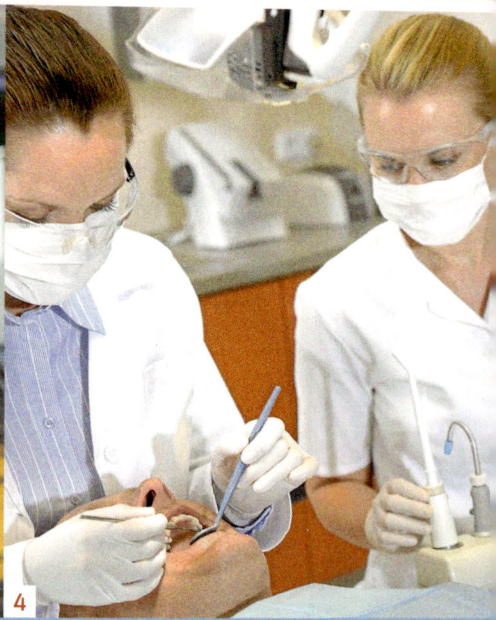
4

Unit 4
Dos and don’ts at work

1 Different jobs, different rules

R **A Look at the pictures on the left and find:**

a shop assistant / a construction worker / a dental assistant / a bus driver

R **B In every job there are 'rules' – things you must (or mustn't) do. Match these rules to the jobs in the four pictures.**

1 Someone in this job must (or: has to) drive carefully. They mustn't drive too fast, for example.
2 In this job, you must (or: have to) be polite to your customers. You mustn't be rude to them! "The customer is always right!"
3 A person in this job must / has to have very clean hands because hygiene is important. (S)he mustn't have dirty fingers.
4 People in this job must / have to wear a hard hat at work. They mustn't work without one.

R, P **C In different jobs there are also different things that aren't so important. The construction worker on the left is Sam. The dental assistant is Katie. Who is this – Sam or Katie?**

1 This person doesn't have to wear a hard hat at work. *That's …*
2 This person doesn't have to have very clean hands.

Tips and tricks

Vorsicht!
you mustn't = du **darfst** nicht
you don't have to = du **musst / brauchst** nicht

M **D Translate the six sentences in exercises B and C above into German. Compare with a partner, then tell the class.**

R, I **E Think about the rules at your college. Finish these sentences in your own words, then talk in class.**

1 At my college, we must / have to …
2 We mustn't …
3 But we don't have to …

→ rule → assistant → hard hat → important

Am Ende von Unit 4 kann ich:

— über Regeln am Arbeitsplatz reden und schreiben,
— Schilder am Arbeitsplatz verstehen,
— über mögliche Konflikte am Arbeitsplatz reden und schreiben.

2 Signs at work

R **A There are lots of signs at work – in offices, in factories, in shops, in car parks, and on construction sites. Look at the signs on the next page. Find a sign or signs …**

1 about something you wear on your ears.
2 about something you wear on your eyes.
3 about smoking.
4 about the floor in a shop.
5 about electricity.
6 for car and lorry drivers.
7 about a construction site.
8 about your bags at an airport.
9 about fire.
10 about a small vehicle that transports heavy things.
11 about mobile (cell) phones.
12 for visitors to an office or a factory.

That's sign C (D, L, …).

R, P **B Make two lists. Which signs say things you *must / have to do* and which signs say things you *mustn't do*?**

must / have to	mustn't
sign N, …	sign A, …

P **C Make sentences about the signs. Use the verbs and phrases below.**

use · smoke · wear · leave · be careful because there is / are … · break · go · park your car · stop · drive faster than

Sign A means you mustn't smoke.

P **D Look at the sign on the right. It's on the noticeboard in an office in the USA. Can you explain – what is 'Casual Friday'? (Tip: you wear 'casual clothes' like jeans and T-shirts at home. In offices, people normally wear 'formal clothes' like suits and skirts.) Think about *must / have to, mustn't* and *don't have to.***

REMEMBER!

TOMORROW IS
CASUAL FRIDAY

→ electricity → lorry → to transport → to break → noticeboard

P **E** **Can you give the missing forms?**

Must* und *have to				→ More please **A – F**
I			have to	don't have to
he she it	must	mustn't	**?**	**?**
we you they			have to	don't have to

→ caution → danger → in case of (fire) → Keep out!

3 Conflicts at work

A 1.16

JOB MAG is a magazine in Britain for young people in their first years at work. There are articles about careers, interviews, news stories ... and much more. There is also a letter page where people can write if they have problems in their workplace. Here are two letters to the Job Mag problem page. Read the letters below and do task A on page 55.

Dear JOB MAG

I am 19 years old and I work as a receptionist in a dental practice in my town. Together with three other women, I work at the reception desk, answer the phone, put appointments into the computer and so on. Because we are a small team, we also have to share lots of other smaller jobs – we make tea and coffee for the dentists, for example, take letters to the post office at the end of the day, sometimes go to the bank for cash – and so on. The problem is that one woman in our team, Judith, is a bit older and thinks she is 'better' than us younger girls. She refuses to do these smaller jobs. I love my work generally but Judith is a real problem for me. Can you help? **Cheryl, Manchester**

Dear JOB MAG

I am a shop assistant in a sports shop in my town. It is part of a big national chain. I started work there last year and at first I loved the job. But then six months ago, I began to get angry about my work and now I am very unhappy. The problem is our manager. There are five assistants in the store and the manager likes two of them and doesn't like the others. I'm one of the assistants he doesn't like! With his two favourites (one of them is the son of the manager's friend) he's always nice and they get all the interesting jobs. On the other hand, the three of us all get the not-so-nice jobs: we have to clean the floor, for example, and move around all big boxes of sports goods. I don't really want to have to look for a new job but at the moment I hate going to work in the shop. Please help! **Robert, Bristol**

→ workplace → appointment → to refuse (to do sth) → chain (of shops)

R, P, I **A** **True or false? Note down T or F, then compare answers in class. When a sentence is wrong, give a correct sentence.**

1 Cheryl is a receptionist and Robert is a shop assistant.
2 Cheryl has a problem with her two young colleagues.
3 Robert's problem is with his shop manager.
4 Judith works well in the team and shares all the work with the others.
5 In Robert's shop, the manager's favourites don't have to do the more difficult jobs.
6 Cheryl doesn't like her work but she likes Judith.
7 Robert plans to look for a new job.

R, P, I A1.17 **B** **Here are the magazine's answers to the two letters. Work with a partner or in a small group. Make 'to-do' lists for Cheryl and Robert according to the magazine. Compare your answers in class.**

Dear Cheryl
It is particularly important in a small office that everyone works together. First, you must talk to your two younger colleagues. If they feel like you (and I think they will!), go and talk to Judith together. Explain how you feel and ask Judith about her feelings. Remember: you mustn't get angry! Problems often happen at work and you can usually solve them if you talk. If Judith still refuses to share jobs, then you must go to the practice manager or one of the dentists.

Dear Robert
I understand why you are unhappy. Usually, it is best to talk to the person who is your 'problem', but in your situation, I think you have to talk to someone who is 'higher' than your boss. Your shop is part of a big, national chain. Write to the head office. They will probably talk to your boss and perhaps to your other colleagues if they are also unhappy. Before you contact the company, you must also write down examples of the things you are unhappy about – what happened, dates etc. The situation in your shop is unfair and you don't have to put up with it.

P, I **EXTRA** **Choose one of the letters. For Cheryl, act out the discussion with Judith. For Robert, write a letter to his head office.**

→ head office → probably → to put up with (sth)

4 More please!

R
A must (have to) / mustn't → Grammar 8
Write down a) or b).

1 In England you a) must b) mustn't drive on the left.
2 But you a) have to b) mustn't drive on the left in Germany!
3 On construction sites, workers usually a) have to b) mustn't wear hard hats.
4 You a) must b) mustn't smoke where you see a 'no smoking' sign.
5 In many offices nowadays, workers a) have to b) mustn't go outside to smoke.
6 Lorry drivers drive long distances. Sometimes they a) have to b) mustn't be away from home for a week or more.
7 Sorry. Customers a) must b) mustn't bring dogs into the shop.
8 Chefs a) have to b) mustn't work in hot kitchens. And often they a) must b) mustn't work in the evenings and at weekends too.

P
B must / has to / doesn't have to → Grammar 8
Finish the text about Ed.

Ed is an office worker in New York. From Monday to Friday he **(1)** ... travel to work on the subway. He **(2)** ... wear a suit and a tie and he **(3)** ... work from 9 a.m. to 5 p.m. in his office. But Saturday and Sunday are different. Ed **(4)** ... travel on the subway and he **(5)** ... wear a suit or a tie. In the summer, he usually goes to the beach on Coney Island. He swims in the sea and relaxes. He **(6)** ... work. It's great!

Office workers 'enjoy' smoking nowadays!

P
C mustn't / don't have to → Grammar 8
Give the missing words.

1 The sign says: 'No parking'. That means you ... park here.
2 This software is free. You ... pay for it.
3 He won 70 million euros on the lottery so he ... work.
4 The meeting starts at 11.00. Be there punctually! You ... be late!
5 Listen carefully. You ... forget this, it's important.
6 You can do that if you want – but you ... You can decide.
7 Mobile phones are forbidden here. Pupils ... use them in class!
8 Companies sometimes say: 'Pay in 30 days.' In other words, customers ... pay immediately.

P

D must (have to) / mustn't / don't have to → Grammar 8

Serkan is from Bochum in Germany. Last month, he finished his business course at college. Now he is in Birmingham, Britain's second largest city. He has a work placement *(Praktikum)* in a British media company. It makes films for TV and sells them around the world. Serkan is in the export department. It is Serkan's first day in the office. Read his job description and the office rules, then say if the sentences below are true or false. When a sentence is false, write a correct sentence. Use *has to, doesn't have to* or *mustn't.*

JOB DESCRIPTION

- Work from 9.00 a.m. to 5.30 p.m. Monday to Friday. Weekends are free.
- Answer the telephone.
- Translate letters and emails from our German customers.
- Write letters and emails in German to our German customers.

OFFICE RULES

Please do ...

- Ties and suits are not necessary but please be dressed smartly at all times.
- Be punctual.
- Turn off your computer at the end of the day.

Please don't ...

- Don't use the office telephone for private calls.
- Don't send or receive personal emails.
- Don't eat at your desk.
- This is a no-smoking office.

1 Serkan has to start work each day at 9 o'clock. *True*
2 He has to work on Saturdays.
False. He doesn't have to work on Saturdays.
3 When the telephone on his desk rings, he has to answer it.
4 Serkan can use the phone on his desk to phone his parents in Germany.
5 He doesn't have to turn off his computer at 5.30.
6 He has to wear a suit and tie at work.
7 He has to write letters to the company's British customers.
8 He mustn't eat sandwiches at his desk.
9 He can smoke in the office.
10 He has to arrive punctually at work each day.
11 He can email his old college friends in Germany from his computer.
12 He has to translate German letters and emails into English.

must (have to) / mustn't / don't have to → Grammar 8

EXTRA Serkan wants to tell his friends in Germany about his job and the rules in his office. Write an email for him in German (which he can send from his own computer of course!).

P ▲ **F must (have to) / mustn't** → Grammar 8

Serkan has his car with him in Birmingham so he has to know about English road signs and traffic lights. Write a sentence about each of these signs. Use the phrases below the signs. Tip: the speed limit *(Geschwindigkeitsbegrenzung)* in British towns is 30 miles per hour (mph).

- This sign means that you …
- When you see this sign you …
- You … when you see this sign / when the traffic lights are …
- you can / you are allowed to …
- you have to / you must …
- you mustn't / you aren't allowed to / it is forbidden to …

P ▲ **G Key words**

Look at the words at the bottom of pages 51–55. Choose the best words to finish the sentences below.

1 … tell you the things you must or mustn't do. One … at my college is 'No smoking in the college'.
2 A … is a large vehicle that transports goods. In German it's called an 'LKW'.
3 When you see the word '…' on a sign, it means you must be careful.
4 In hotels, you often see the sign: 'Don't use the lift … … … fire'. That means you mustn't use it when there is a fire.
5 If you see a sign on a door that says: '… …!' it means you mustn't go into that room.
6 (Man to receptionist in an office) 'Good morning. I have an … with Ms Westbury at 10.30.'
7 McDonalds is an international … of fast food restaurants.
8 'No! I … to do that!'
9 We have offices around the UK but our … … is in London.
10 You don't have to … … … things in your workplace that are unfair! Talk or write to someone about the situation.

5 Now you

I, P **A Being a college student is very different from working in a job. Work with a partner or in a small group and do the tasks below. Then compare your answers in class and talk about college and working.**

1 Write down two things you have to do at college but that you don't have to do when you have a job.
2 Write down two things you maybe have to do when you have a job but that you don't have to do when you are a student.
3 Write down one reason why being at college is perhaps better than having a job.
4 Write down one reason why having a job is perhaps better than being at college.
5 What do you think? Which is better? College or a job? Why?

V4

Video Lounge Working as a PA

A PA is a Personal Assistant. Jasmine Goodman is a PA in the same firm as Sally (Unit 2). She works for Ms Kennedy. She is looking after the two visitors. They are in Ms Kennedy's office.

R, P **Watch the video and answer the questions.**

1 Ms Kennedy is not there. Why not?
2 Jasmine offers the visitors something to drink while they are waiting. What drinks do they choose?
3 One of the visitors tells Jasmine that she doesn't have to call him Mr Rogers. What can Jasmine call him?
4 Jasmine says to the visitors that she is sorry they have to ... (what?). How do they reply?

LOCAL SUCCESS STORY

Do you need a plumber? What about new windows? A patio in your garden maybe? Then ring Lucas Nowak.

A 1.18

Lucas is from Poland – his real name is Lukasz. But he has lived in Danbury since 2008. And he has had his own building firm here for three years.

"When I first came to England," says Lucas "I wanted to stay maybe a year or two just to earn some money. But now I want to stay in Danbury. The people are very friendly and my new life here is very good."

LUCAS NOWAK has been in Danbury since 2008 – and he wants to stay.

Unit 5
Success stories

1 A new life

R, P **A Read about Lukasz and answer the questions.**

Lukasz Nowak was born in Poland. But in 2008, when he was 24, he moved to England. He now lives in a town in England called Danbury. Lukasz worked in Danbury first as a plumber. Then three years ago, he started his own small building firm. He now has six employees. His firm is very successful. Everybody in Danbury knows 'Lucas'.

1 Where was Lukasz born?
2 When did he move to England? What town does he live in?
3 What was Lukasz's first job in Danbury?
4 What did he do three years ago?

Hier und dort

Großbritannien ist ein multikulturelles Land – in London werden über 300 verschiedene Sprachen gesprochen. In den 1960er Jahren wanderten viele Menschen aus Indien, Pakistan, China oder der Karibik ein. Seit 2004 gibt es auch viele Einwanderer aus Mitteleuropa – wie Lukasz.

R **B The article on the left is from the local newspaper in Danbury. Look at it now and find the missing verbs for the diagram below.**

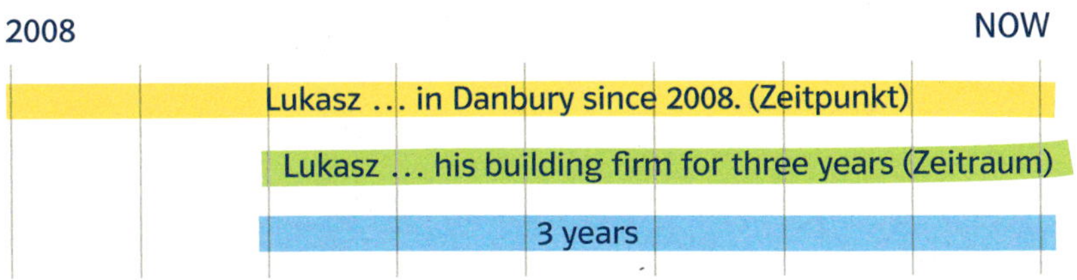

Lucasz has … since …
He has … for …

Tips and tricks

since 2008 = Zeitpunkt
for three years = Zeitraum
Vorsicht! Auf Deutsch heißen *since* und *for* beide ‚seit'!

M **C Your friend wants to know about the article but (s)he doesn't speak English. Give the most important ideas in German.**

→ to move → (his) own (firm) → employee → local
→ to earn (money)

Am Ende von Unit 5 kann ich:

– mitteilen, seit wann etwas schon andauert,
– über Erfolgsgeschichten reden und schreiben.

2 A magazine article

R A1.19

A Read this magazine article about a famous British chef. Find out …

1 Why was Jamie no good at school?
2 Who are the young people with Jamie in the photo at the top?
3 Who is the woman with him in the second photo?

No good at school but great at his job

Jamie Oliver makes cooking cool. He's famous now and he's often on TV – and not just in Britain but around the world. But Jamie wasn't a good pupil at school! Here's his success story.

Jamie and Jools

Jamie was born in the south-east of England in 1975. His mum and dad had a pub and Jamie started helping in the kitchen there when he was eight. School was hard for Jamie – he's dyslexic – but after school, when he was 16, he went to a college in London and trained to be a chef. Jamie was a brilliant college student. He left college in 1992. He worked in some famous restaurants in France, and then in London. In 1998, a British TV company made a film about one of the London restaurants. Everybody saw Jamie on TV and soon he was the star of the show. Jamie Oliver, the unsuccessful pupil, was famous!

Jamie opened his first restaurant in London in 2002 – but it wasn't a normal restaurant. He found 15 unemployed young people and trained them. The young people had lots of problems and it was hard work, but they were successful. They are now chefs in the restaurant. The restaurant is called *Fifteen* because there were 15 young chefs. Then Jamie trained more young people in England, Holland and Australia.

Jamie is married. He met his wife Juliette (Jamie calls her 'Jools') at school. He married her in 2000. They live in London and have four children.

→ to train to be a … → chef → to leave (college) → unemployed → dyslexic

R **B** **Which is right? Note down a, b or c.**

1 Jamie Oliver was born
  a in the north of England.
  b in the south-west of England.
  c in the south-east of England.
2 He first worked in a kitchen
  a at school.
  b in his parents' pub.
  c at college.
3 Jamie trained to be a chef
  a in London.
  b in France.
  c in the USA.
4 He was first on TV
  a in 1975.
  b in 1987.
  c in 1998.
5 Jamie trained 15 … people for his *Fifteen* restaurant in London.
  a successful young
  b unemployed old
  c unemployed young
6 Jamie now has *Fifteen* restaurants in … countries.
  a two
  b three
  c four
7 Jamie first met his wife … and they have …
  a in 2000 / three children.
  b at college / two children.
  c at school / four children.

P **C** **Finish the *How long …?* sentences about Jamie.**

Then	Now	How long …?
1 Jamie first worked as a chef in 1992.	He works as a chef now.	He *has* worked as a chef *since* 1992.
2 Jamie was first famous in 1998.	He's famous now.	He … been famous … 1998.
3 Jamie had his first *Fifteen* restaurant in London in 2002.	He has a *Fifteen* restaurant in London now.	He … a *Fifteen* restaurant in London … 2002.
4 He had his first *Fifteen* restaurant in Australia in 2006.	He has a *Fifteen* restaurant in Australia now.	He has had a *Fifteen* restaurant in Australia for … years.
5 Jamie married Jools in 2000.	He's married to Jools now.	He has been married to Jools … years.

I **D** **Ask and answer questions with a partner like those on the right.**

How long has Jamie Oliver worked as a chef?

He has worked as a chef since …

How long has he …?

He has …

P **E** **Can you give the missing forms?**

Das present perfect → More please **A – E**

I	have	worked been lived had
he / she / it	?	
we you they	?	

→ successful → to marry → to be married to (someone)

3 We have our own firm!

R **A Read about Kate, Annie and Ruth.**

1 Where do they live?
2 Where were they all students?
3 What did they do after college?
4 What does their firm do?

Ruth

Kate and Annie

Kate, Annie and Ruth live in Danbury in England – the same town as Lukasz Nowak. They were all students – and best friends – at Danbury FE college. When they left college, they started their own firm in the town. It's called PartyPeople. The firm organises parties (with food and music) for schools, local firms and local kids.

R, P A 1.20 **B A reporter from the Danbury newspaper is interviewing Kate, Annie and Ruth about their firm. He has these questions for them. Listen and find the answers.**

Questions for Kate, Annie and Ruth
1 How old are you?
2 What courses were you on at college?
3 How long have you had the firm 'PartyPeople'?
4 What are your different jobs in the firm?
5 How (where etc.) did you start the firm?
6 How long have you been in your office?

→ cookery → electronics → customer

R, P **C** **You're the reporter now. Finish your article about Kate, Annie and Ruth.**

Three Danbury women and their successful company

Do you want a party? Do you need food? Music? The local firm PartyPeople can organise everything for you!

Kate, Annie and Ruth are now **(1)** ... years old. They were all friends and students at **(2)** ... College. Kate was on a **(3)** ... course, Annie on a **(4)** ... course and Ruth wanted to be a **(5)** ... When they left college, they started their firm, PartyPeople. They have had the firm now for **(6)** ... years.

The three women all have different jobs in the company. **(7)** ... is the 'businesswoman', **(8)** ... is the disk jockey who plays the music, and **(9)** ... cooks all the food for the parties.

PartyPeople is very successful now. But it was small when it started. At first, Kate, Annie and Ruth organised the parties and cooked the food in Kate's **(10)** ... Now the three women use an old pizzeria in Danbury. They cook the food in the kitchen and the **(11)** ... is their office. They have been in the pizzeria for **(12)** ... years.

I, P **D** **Interview your partner.** ⟶ More please! F

1 First copy and fill in the form for YOU.
2 Then interview a partner. Write in your partner's answers.
3 Write a short text about your partner.

My partner ... (name) *lives in* ... *(S)he's lived there for / since* ...

	YOU	Your partner
1 What street do you live in? How long have you lived there?	?	?
2 What's your favourite band? How long have you liked it?	?	?
3 What's your favourite piece of clothing? How long have you had it?	?	?
4 Do you have a car, a bike or a scooter? How long have you had it?	?	?
5 How long have you learned English?	?	?

So läuft's besser
Für das *present perfect* brauchst du noch die unregelmäßigen Verben im Klappumschlag. Dieses Mal geht es um die 3. Form:
to be – was / were – ***been***
to go – went – ***gone***

⟶ to organise ⟶ to fill in a form ⟶ piece of clothing

4 More please!

P △ **A since / for** → Grammar 4

***Since* or *for*? Finish the sentences.**

1 Lukasz Nowak has lived in England ... 2008.
2 He has had his own firm ... the last 3 years.
3 Jamie Oliver has been a famous chef ... over 20 years.
4 He has been married to Jools ... 2000.
5 Greg is an English college student. He has been at college ... last September.
6 He's at college now. He has been there ... 9.00 this morning.
7 It's midday now so he has been there ... 3 hours.

P ▲ **B Present perfect with since / for** → Grammar 4

Answer the questions with complete sentences.
Be careful with *since* and *for*!

1 How long has Lukasz Nowak lived in England? (2008)
He (Lukasz) has lived in England since 2008.
2 How long has Jamie Oliver been a chef? (over 20 years)
3 How long have you been married, Jamie? (2000)
I ...
4 How long have Jamie and Jools lived in London? (12 years)
5 How long have you worked in a *Fifteen* restaurant, Laura? (2011)
6 How long has David been a chef? (3 years)

He's been a chef for three years but before that he worked in a circus.

P △ **C Present perfect / simple present / simple past** → Grammar 1, 3, 4

In sentences a), b) and c), one verb is in the *simple present*, one in the *simple past*, and one in the *present perfect*. Give the right forms.

1 a Lukasz *lives* (live) in Danbury.
b He *moved* (move) to Danbury in 2008.
c He ... (live) in Danbury since 2008.

2 a Jamie Oliver ... (leave) college in 1992.
b He ... (be) a chef now.
c He ... (be) a chef since 1992.

3 a Laura ... (be) a chef in a *Fifteen* restaurant.
b She ... (start) working there 18 months ago.
c She ... (worked) there now for 18 months.

Name:	Nadine Zimmermann
Age:	19
Born:	Krefeld, Germany
Family:	Father Rolf, Mother Angelika
3 years ago:	Family left Krefeld and moved to St. Louis, Missouri, USA. Father got job as police officer
Last year:	Nadine finished high school in St. Louis and became a student on a business course at a community college there
Six months ago:	Mother got a job as a nurse in hospital in St. Louis. Nadine met Ben, (her "true love"!), another student on her course

R, P ▲

D Present perfect / simple present / simple past → Grammar 1, 3, 4

I live in America now! Read the 'quick facts' about Nadine and answer the questions below. Be careful to use the right tenses!

1 Where was Nadine born? *She …*
2 Where does she live now?
3 When did she leave Germany?
4 What city in the USA did she move to?
5 What is her father's job there?
6 How long has he had that job?
7 What is her mother's job?
8 How long has she had that job?
9 What kind of school did Nadine go to first in St. Louis?
10 Where is Nadine a student now and what course is she on?
11 How long has she been a student there?
12 How long has Nadine known Ben? Why is he important in her life?

R, P ▲

E Present perfect / simple present / simple past (negatives) → Grammar 1, 3, 4

Look again at the quick facts about Nadine and say if the sentences below are true (T) or false (F). Correct the false sentences.

1 Nadine has been Ben's girlfriend for three years.
False! She hasn't … . She …
2 She moved to the States last year.
3 Her dad works in a hospital in St. Louis.
4 Her mum has been a nurse for six months.
5 Nadine is on a sports and leisure course.
6 She doesn't like Ben very much.
7 Nadine became a student on her course two years ago.

F Present perfect / simple present / simple past → Grammar 1, 3, 4

A1.21

The world skateboarding championship is in Germany next week. Here is an interview with Andy Lewis, the world champion at the moment. Read the interview and do task 1 or 2 below.

Interviewer Hi Andy and thanks for this interview.
Andy No problem.
Interviewer OK, first some questions about you. How old are you and where were you born?
Andy I'm 21 and I was born in Boston, Massachusetts, in the USA.
Interviewer When did you start skateboarding?
Andy When I was a junior at high school, when I was 12.
Interviewer Did you know then that you wanted to be a professional skateboarder?
Andy No, not at first. It was just fun. But then when I was about 16, I took part in a competition and I won. I thought: "This is great! I can earn money like this!"
Interviewer When did you become a pro?
Andy After high school, when I was 18, I left Boston and moved to California. I became a pro then.
Interviewer How long have you been world champion?
Andy For two years now. I won my first world championship in Japan two years ago.
Interviewer How often do you train?
Andy I usually train about six hours every day.
Interviewer Wow! That's a lot!
Andy Sure, but if you want to be world champion, you have to work hard!

P △ **1 Write six sentences about Andy. Use the *simple present* in two sentences, the *simple past* in two and the *present perfect* in the last two:**

Andy is the world champion at the moment. (simple present).
He started … (simple past) He has … (present perfect).

P ▲ **2 You are a journalist and this is your interview with Andy. Write a short article about him (100 words). Find a good headline for your article.**

G Key words

M ▲ **Look at the key words at the bottom of pages 61–65 and translate the sentences below into English.**

1 Sie haben ihre eigene Firma.
2 Wenn du einen Job hast, verdienst du Geld – das ist klasse!
3 Zur Zeit hat sie keinen Job - sie ist arbeitslos.
4 Er ist seit 10 Jahren ein erfolgreicher Sänger.
5 Bitte fügen Sie in das Formular Name und Adresse ein.

5 Now you

R, P, I **A** **Work with a partner. You are two college students who are chatting online. One of you is from another country – England, the USA etc. This is your first chat so you want to find out about each other. Think of screen names for yourselves. First, complete the sentences below, then continue your chat. Use your own ideas.**

Partner A (You live e.g. in the States.) What town do you live in Germany?
Partner B I live in … What about you? Where do you live?
Partner A I …
Partner B How long have you lived there?
Partner A I have … What about you? How long …?
Partner B …

P, I **B** **Work in small groups. Choose one of the tasks below and give a short talk to the class.**

1 Did you, your family or someone you know move to Germany from another country? When? What happened?
How long have you lived in Germany now? What are your ideas about Germany?
2 Do you know a success story? It can be a famous person, someone in your family, someone you know or a friend. Tell the story.

V5

Video Lounge Introducing people

R, P, I **In Unit 4 you met Jasmine, Ms Kennedy's PA. This is Ms Kennedy. She is now in her office. Jasmine is introducing Ms Kennedy to the two visitors, Mr Carter and Mr Rogers. Watch the video. Write down the missing words from these phrases. Then make a small group. Try the conversation yourselves.**

1 I'd like to … John Carter and Paul Rogers.
2 … to meet you!
3 Please, … me Diane.
4 This is my … Paul Rogers.
5 (Diane) I'm … I'm late.
6 (John) Oh, don't … Jasmine took care of us.
7 Please have a … (= please sit down).

WORK EXPERIENCE PLACEMENT
3 – 14 September

Apple Tree Nursery

We are offering a two-week work experience placement in our busy nursery. It will be suitable for a FULL-TIME STUDENT.

Hours: Daily from 9 am to 5 pm Monday to Friday.
Pay: Students will work as volunteers (no pay) but we will give you travel expenses and lunch each day.

Interested? Apply now! Send an email and your CV to: katybrand@appletreenursery.co.uk

Good luck and we hope to meet you soon!

A 1.23

Unit 6
Work experience

1 Looking for work experience

R, P **A Read about Paul. Answer the questions below.**

A1.22

Paul is a student at a college of further education (an FE college) in London, England. His course lasts two years and Paul is now near the end of his first year. After college he wants to be a nursery assistant and it will be very good for him if he can get some work experience first. This morning, he's looking at an advertisement on the noticeboard in his college.

1 What do you learn in the text about Paul and his college?
2 What is Paul doing in the picture on the left?
3 Why is he perhaps interested in the advertisement?

M **B Look at the ad on the noticeboard on the left. Find the English words and phrases for:**

Freiwillige · Praktikum · es ist geeignet für · Lebenslauf · Bewerben Sie sich jetzt! · wir bieten an · Reisekosten

R, P, I **C Work with a partner then report to the class. Look at the ad again. True or false? Can you correct the false sentences?**

1 If Paul gets the work experience in the nursery, it will last one week.
2 He will work five days a week.
3 He won't earn any money.
4 If he goes to the nursery by bus, he will pay for the bus himself.

Am Ende von Unit 6 kann ich:

— mich um ein Praktikum bewerben und über meinen Lebenslauf sprechen und schreiben,
— sagen, was passieren wird, wenn …

→ work experience (placement) → ad(vertisement)
→ to be suitable (for) → to apply for sth → CV

2 Looking at ads

R, P, I **A Two big, international German companies are offering work experience. They want students who can speak English, so the ads are in English! Work with a partner.**

PARTNER A: Please go now to page 81.
PARTNER B: 1 Look at your ad below. Copy and complete the table with information from your ad.
2 Next, answer your partner's questions about your ad.
3 Then, ask your partner questions and complete the table about her / his ad. The phrases on the right will help you.

What company will you work for?

What will the placement be – what job will you do?

Where …? / When …?

Will you need English?

What hours / days will you …?

Will you get any pay – will you earn any money?

KARL BOSSMANN

WORK EXPERIENCE

SALES ASSISTANT, BERLIN

KARL BOSSMANN is Germany's biggest retailer of fashion clothing for men and women. We are now offering a work experience placement in our store in Berlin.
It will be suitable for a full-time student and will be for one week from Monday 12 – Saturday 17 October. If you get the placement, you will work from 8 am to 6 pm each day. Our Berlin store gets many international customers so you will often need English. The placement is unpaid but you will learn a lot in a big, international company like ours. For more information, phone us on (030) 414 71 86 or email us at karl.bossmann.de.
We hope to hear from you soon!

	My ad	My partner's ad
Company	Karl Bossmann	?
Placement (job)	sales …	?
Place of work	?	?
Dates	?	?
Knowledge of English	?	?
Hours	?	?
Pay?	?	?

→ retailer → place of work → knowledge (of English)

You **won't get** any pay
with the company,
but you **will get**
lunch in the cafeteria.

R, P, I **B** **With your partner again, compare the two placements. Finish the sentences below.**

1 If you get the placement with Karl Bossmann, you *will be* (be) a sales assistant.
2 If you *get* (get) the placement with Deutsche Mobil, you will be a secretary.
3 If you get the placement with Karl Bossmann, you ... (work) in ... (city).
4 If you ... (get) the placement with Deutsche Mobil, you ... (work) in ... (city).
5 If you work in the Karl Bossmann store, you ... (need) English every day.
6 You ... (use) English if you ... (work) in the Deutsche Mobil office in Münster, too.
7 You ... (work) for one week if you ... (get) the placement with Karl Bossmann.
8 But you ... (get) two week's work experience if you ... (be) with Deutsche Mobil.
9 You won't get any pay if you ... (work) for Karl Bossmann – but you will learn a lot!
10 You ... (not get) any pay with Deutsche Mobil – but they ... (give) you your lunch in the cafeteria every day.

P **C** **Can you give the missing forms – *will (won't)* or *simple present?***

If-Sätze Typ 1	→ More please! **A – F**
If you ... (work) in Berlin,	you ... (be) a sales assistant.
You ... (be) a secretary	if you ... (work) in Münster.
You ... (not/get) any pay	if you work in Berlin.
If you ... (work) in Münster	you ... (not get) any pay but you ... (get) your lunch.

→ cafeteria → lunch → to need English (in a job)

3 Applying for a placement

R, P **A This is Stephanie Holler, from Germany. Below, you can see her CV (Curriculum Vitae). Read the CV and answer the questions about Stephanie.**

1 What German city is she from?
2 She is a college student at the moment. At which college?
3 What qualification did she get from her secondary school?
4 Which computer programs does she know?
5 What foreign language does she speak?
6 What does Stephanie like doing in her free time?
7 What part-time job has she had since 2012?

CURRICULUM VITAE

PERSONAL DETAILS

Name:	Stephanie Holler
Address:	Altendorferstraße 12 45143 Essen, Germany
Date of birth:	30.10.1996

EDUCATION AND QUALIFICATIONS

Primary school:	2002–2007	Schule am Postleitweg
Sedondary school	2007–2012	Hauptschule Gervinus Qualification: Hauptschulabschluss
Vocational college	2012–	Berufskolleg Essen (Berufsfachschule)

WORK EXPERIENCE

2012–	Part-time job at City Hotel, Essen (waitress)

SKILLS:

Computer:	Microsoft Word, Microsoft Excel, Social Media
Languages:	German (mother tongue); English (good)

INTERESTS	All types of sport, playing the guitar, reading, internet

→ education → qualification → primary / secondary school
→ skill(s) → mother tongue

R, P, I
A1.24

B Stephanie would like to have some work experience – and a placement in England would be great! She sees this ad on a website. With a partner, write a short text about what will happen if Stephanie gets this placement. Then report to the class. Begin like this:

If Stehanie gets this placement, she will work in a big London hotel for four weeks from …

M
A1.25

C With some help from her friends and her English teacher at college, Stephanie writes the email below and attaches her CV. How does she say these things in her email? → More please! G – I

Ich hänge meinen Lebenslauf an. · Ich würde mich sehr über die Chance, in London zu arbeiten, freuen. · Zur Zeit bin ich Vollzeitschülerin. · Ich bin lernwillig. · Ich schreibe, um mich um … zu bewerben. · Ich werde meine Schule nächsten Sommer abschließen. · Mit freundlichen Grüßen · Sehr geehrte Frau Richards

Dear Ms Richards

I am writing to apply for the work experience placement which you advertised on the Praktika.eu website.

I am currently a full-time student at a vocational college in Essen, Germany. I will complete my course in summer next year. I attach my CV.

For the last year I have worked part-time at a large, international hotel in Essen. I am keen to learn, work hard, and my English is good. I would very much welcome the chance to work for you in London.

I look forward to hearing from you.

Yours sincerely
Stephanie Holler

→ to advertise (a job) → to attach sth (to an email) → currently
→ Yours sincerely

ONE MONTH'S WORK EXPERIENCE IN LONDON!

The HORSEGUARDS HOTEL in London is offering a work experience placement for a full-time student from the EU. The placement is unpaid but the hotel will provide a room and meals. Sorry, we cannot pay travel expenses to and from London. If you get the placement, you will work in many different areas of the hotel including at the reception desk and in the restaurant. The placement will be from 1 – 30 October. Interested? Email Debbie Richards with your CV at: d.richards@horseguardshotel.co.uk

4 More please!

M ▲ **A Useful words**

Give the missing English words and phrases in the sentences.

1 A *work experience placement* (Praktikum) is a great way to learn about a job.
2 You can often find ... (Anzeigen) for these in magazines or on the internet.
3 For example, this company ... (bietet) work experience in a big store.
4 The placement ... (eignet sich) for students who are at college ... (vollzeit).
5 People in a work experience placement don't usually get any ... (Lohn / Bezahlung).
6 This company also wants to know about your ... (Englisch-kenntnisse).
7 If you are interested in the placement, you can ask for more ... (Informationen) by phone or by email.

P ▲ **B *If*-Sätze Typ 1** → Grammar 9

Finish the sentences with the correct forms of the verbs – the *simple present* or *will*.

1 If you *work* here, you ... (learn) a lot about life in a big store.
2 You ... (learn) a lot about life in a big store if you ... (work) here.
3 If you ... (like) big cities, you ... (love) Berlin.
4 If a British or American customer ... (come) into the store, you ... (need) to speak English.
5 If Stefan ... (get) the work placement in this company, he ... (work) in one of their offices.
6 He ... (work) there for two weeks if he ... (get) the placement.
7 He ... (use) his English on the phone if a British customer calls the office.
8 I think that if he ... (use) his English a lot, it ... (become) better.

"We give all our work experience students help with their travel."

P ▲ **C *If*-Sätze Typ 1: Verneinung** → Grammar 9

All the sentences below are wrong. Correct each sentence with two new ones.

1 You will earn €1,000 a month if you work here. (€100)
(No!) You won't earn €1,000 a month if you work here. You will earn €100 a month.
2 Veronika will work in Berlin if she gets the placement. (Frankfurt)
(No!) She ...
3 If she works for that company, she will get a free lunch every day. (€ 20 a week for meals)
4 If she works there, she will get travel expenses. (pay for travel herself)

VMW WORK EXPERIENCE

VMW is Germany's biggest manufacturer of cars and trucks. We are now **(1)** ... work experience **(2)** ... in our repair workshops across Germany. These placements will be **(3)** ... for FULL-TIME students. All will be for two **(4)** ... from 3–14 September. If you get one of the placements, you will work **(5)** ... 8 am **(6)** ... 4 pm. each day, Monday to Friday. The placements are unpaid – that means you won't get any **(7)** ... – but you will learn a lot from our experts, and we will give you **(8)** ... (Reisegeld) and lunch each day. Interested? For more **(9)** ..., **(10)** ... our programme director Mr Klaus Wenger at k.wenger@vmw.de. Good luck and we **(11)** ... to hear from you soon!

P ▲ **D Useful words**

Give the missing words and phrases in the ad above. All the vocabulary you need is on pages 71–75.

P ▲ **E *If*-Sätze Typ 1** → Grammar 9

Write sentences about the work experience placements in D above. Use *if*-sentences type 1. Be careful with commas!

1 if / you / get / one of the placements / you / work / in a repair workshop
If you get one of the placements, you ...
2 you / work / from Monday to Friday / if / you / get / a placement
3 if / you / get / a placement / you / work / from 8 am to 4 pm.
4 if / you / travel to work / by bus / VMW / pay / for the bus journey
5 you / also / get / lunch / every day / if / you / get / a placement
6 if / you / email / Mr Wenger / he / give / you / more information

Tips and tricks

Wenn ein *if*-Satz mit *if* beginnt, muss ein Komma zwischen die beiden Teilsätze gesetzt werden. Du brauchst kein Komma, wenn der *if*-Satz an zweiter Stelle steht.
→ Grammar 9A

P ▲ **F *If*-Sätze Typ 1 (Verneinung)** → Grammar 9

Looking at the ad in D above again, say if the sentences below are true (T) or false (F). When a sentence is false, correct it with two new sentences. Example:

You will work in England if you get one of these placements.
(F) You won't work in England if ... You will ...

1 If you get a VMW placement, you will receive €100 a week for your work.
2 If you get a placement, you will work in VMW's factory in southern Germany.
3 You won't get lunch if you work for VMW.
4 But you will get your travel expenses if you work for them.
5 Mr Wenger will give you a placement if you email him.
6 If you get a work placement with VMW, they will guarantee you a full-time job after college.

M

G Useful words (Curriculum Vitae)

Copy and complete the table below.

English	German
personal details	(1) …
(2)	Fähigkeiten
education	(3)
(4) …	Grundschule
vocational college	(5) …
(6) …	Anschrift
(7) …	Muttersprache

P, M

H Useful words (email)

Give the missing English words in the phrases, then translate the whole phrase into German.

1 I am writing … … for the work placement which you … on the Praktika.de website.
2 I … my CV to this email.
3 I … … to hearing from you soon.
4 I am … (= now, at the moment) a full-time student at a vocational college in Germany.
5 I work hard and am … to learn (= I want to learn).
6 … Mr Smith (at the beginning of the email / letter).
7 Yours … (at the end).

R, M

I Useful words

Which words and phrases belong to a CV and which to an email? Make two lists, then translate all the words and phrases into German.

1 education and qualifications
2 Dear Mr Smith
3 I am writing to apply for …
4 primary school
5 skills
6 … which you advertised
7 I look forward to hearing from you
8 I am keen to learn
9 date of birth
10 Yours sincerely
11 personal details
12 interests
13 I would welcome the chance to work for you
14 I am currently a student

R, P

J Key words

Look at the key words at the bottom of pages 71–75. Which can you find below? Write out the words and phrases, then choose three and write a sentence with each one.

KNOWLEDGEOFENGLISHLUNCHTOADVERTISEAJOBQUALIFI
CATIONPLACEOFWORKSKILLSCURRENTLYTOATTACHYOURCV
CAFETERIAEDUCATION

Now you

R, P, I **A Work in groups first to write an ad for a work experience placement, then to write a CV and an email (or letter) of application.**

1 Write an ad. The work placement can be in Germany or abroad – but, of course, it must be in English! Think about:
- what firm / job?
- when?
- hours
- pay / travel expenses / …?
- more information?

2 Now exchange your ad with another group.
- write your CV
- write a letter or email of application.

EXTRA Put up your ads, CVs and applications on the classroom wall or noticeboard. Organise a gallery walk. → Skills 16

V6

Video Lounge Meeting a star

It is the three British students' last day in Hollywood. Watch the video.

1 Make small groups (2–4 people).
2 Copy the table below, then make notes in the three columns.
3 Compare your notes in your group. Add new information or correct your notes.
4 One student in your group reports to the class.

Greg and Bob Quickpayne	Maya in casting	The 3 students in the movie at the end

Partner files
Job pages
Test

PARTNER FILES

Unit 3 [5 Now you]

A Ask your partner questions to find the missing facts in this article. Then answer your partner's questions.

The man's name is (1) …. He invented the modern mobile phone. He tested it for the first time on 3 April 1973. On that day, he made the first phone call in New York. (2) … years later, the (3) … company produced the first commercial mobile phones – mobile phones that everyone could buy. They didn't have text messaging or cameras. They weighed over (4) …! And in today's money they cost around $4,000.

Unit 6 [2 Looking at ads]

A 1 Look at your ad below. Copy and complete the table with information from your ad.
2 Next, ask your partner questions and complete the table about her/his ad. The phrases on the right will help you.
3 Then, answer your partner's questions about your ad.

What company will you work for?

What will the placement be – what job will you do?

Where …? / When …?

Will you need English?

What hours / days will you …?

Will you get any pay – will you earn any money?

DEUTSCHE MOBIL // WORK EXPERIENCE 12-23 OCTOBER

SECRETARY, MÜNSTER

Deutsche Mobil is not only one of Germany's biggest companies but also one of the world's most important telecommunications companies. We are now offering a two-week work experience placement in our office in Münster. If you get the placement, you will work from 8.30 am to 4 pm Monday to Friday each week. The work is voluntary (there is no pay) but we will give you lunch each day in our cafeteria. The placement will be suitable for a full-time college student. You will also need good English. Interested? Call us now on 05192 100500 or email us at deutschemobil.de.

	My ad	**My partner's ad**
Company	Deutsche Mobil	?
Placement (job)	secretary	?
Place of work	?	?
Dates	?	?
Knowledge of English	?	?
Hours	?	?
Pay?	?	?

Ceyda

Dominik and Verena

JOB PAGES

Emails at work (Unit 1)

In today's world, everybody uses emails at work. Dominik works for a big German construction firm. He often works on projects with people from other countries. Verena works in a German hairdressing salon but the salon buys lots of products from the UK and the USA. And Ceyda works for a German media company. She writes every day to people around the world. Below you can see three of their emails. Look at them now and do the tasks on page 83.

To: p.smith@londonarchitects.co.uk
Subject: building plans

Hi Paul
Could you please send me a copy of the plans for the next phase of the building? Thanks in advance!
Best wishes
Dominik

To: dave.edwards@hairandbeauty.co.uk
Subject: price list

Dear Dave
Do you have a complete price list for your new hair colour products? We like them very much!
Kind regards
Verena

To: m.lieberman@nyarts.com
Subject: film festival dates

Hey Molly
Hope you're well. Could you please send me the dates of next year's New York Film Festival? Many thanks!
Ceyda

R, P **A** **Below are the replies that Dominik, Verena and Ceyda got to their emails – but they are not in the right order. Match the replies and the emails, then write out the replies below in full.**

Hi ...
Thanks for your email. We're pleased you like our new colours! Here is the price list which you wanted. Let me know if I can help further.
Best wishes
...

Hey ...!
The dates are June 17-23. I'm well, thanks and hope you are too! See you at the festival maybe!
Kind regards
...

Dear ...
Attached are the plans you asked for. Please let me know if you have any further questions.
All the best
...

Hier und dort

In Großbritannien und in den USA sind E-Mails auf der Arbeit oft kurz und umgangssprachlich. Die Kollegen, die regelmäßig miteinander korrespondieren, sprechen sich für gewöhnlich mit ihren Vornamen an. Allerdings ist die Sprache trotzdem höflich, also achte darauf, dass du *please* und *thank you* sagst und höfliche Ausdrücke wie *Could you ...?* verwendest.

M, I **B** **Here are some phrases that you often use in emails at work. Work with a partner. Copy and complete the table with German translations. Compare your answers in class.**

Beginning your email		**Replying**	
Dear / Hi / Hey	*Liebe / r / ...*	Here is / are the ... which you wanted	*Hier ist / sind ...*
Hope you're well		Attached is / are ...	
Could you please send me ...?		(Please) let me know if you have any further questions / if I can help further	
Do you have ...?		Best wishes / Kind regards	
Many thanks / Thanks in advance		All the best	

R, P, I **C** **Now YOU! In class, brainstorm some ideas for emails at work – use the emails above as models. Then in groups, write emails. Exchange these with another group and write replies to their emails. Think of dates, times, names etc. yourselves.**

Travelling for work (Unit 2)

Agnieszka is a health care worker. She works in a care home for the elderly in Germany but next month she has the chance to visit a care home in England. It is in Ashford in the south-east of the country. Agnieszka plans to travel to Ashford by train, but while she is there she needs a cheap hotel for four nights. She looks online and finds the two hotels below. Look at the information about the two hotels and do the tasks on page 85.

ASHFORD LODGE Ashford centre

Ashford Lodge is in the centre of the small town of Ashford and only 20 minutes from Ashford International Railway Station. There are 10 single rooms and 5 double rooms plus one family room (2 adults + 2 children). All rooms have a bathroom and shower. Other facilities include:

- Bar (evenings)
- Free parking
- TV
- Wi-Fi Internet

Please note that we are a non-smoking hotel.

£45 per night incl. breakfast

THE COTTAGE HOTEL Ashford 1.5 miles

The Cottage Hotel is a small, quiet and friendly hotel only one and a half miles from Ashford town. It has 3 single and 2 double rooms. All rooms have their own bathroom and shower, plus TV and tea/coffee making facilities. Parking at the hotel is free. The price of the rooms includes a full English breakfast and we can also serve an evening meal – please book your meal in the morning. There is a good local bus service to and from Ashford.

Please note: sorry, no pets!

£57 per night incl. breakfast

R, P **A Copy the chart and complete it with information about the two hotels, then answer the questions below. Explain your answers.**

	Ashord Lodge	The Cottage Hotel
Location	*Ashford centre*	
Price		
Number of rooms		
Facilities		
Things to note?		

1 Which hotel is nearer to the town of Ashford?
The ... (hotel) because it is ... (and the other hotel is ...)
2 Which hotel is cheaper?
3 Which hotel is bigger?
4 Which hotel gives you breakfast?
5 Can you get an evening meal at both hotels?
You can ... but you can't ...
6 Can you use a computer at both hotels?
7 You want to make tea and coffee in your room.
Which hotel is better?

I, P **B Talk to a partner. Which hotel do you think is better for Agnieszka? Why?**

R, I, P **C Agnieszka chooses the Ashford Lodge and she phones the hotel to book a room. Read the dialogue aloud with a partner. Then write and read out a second (different) phone call – phone The Cottage Hotel, for example. Think of dates, names, rooms etc. yourself.**

Receptionist **Agnieska**

Ashford Lodge, George speaking, how may I help you?
Good morning. I'd like to book a room, please.
Certainly. When would you like to stay?
For four nights from the 8th to the 12th of January.
One moment, please. Is that a single or a double room?
A single.
Yes, that's fine. Can I take your name?
Yes, it's Kowalski, that's K-O-W-A- L-S-K-I. Initial A for Agnieszka.
Thank you very much, Ms Kowalski. So that's a single room for four nights from the 8th to the 12th of January. We look forward to seeing you then.
Thanks very much. Goodbye.
You're welcome. Bye now.

A company profile (Unit 3)

Many German companies are famous around the world. 'Made in Germany' means good quality! One of these international companies is Heller AG. If you have a car, a lorry or even a motorbike, then there is a chance that on it you have a Heller product. Below you can see a profile of the company. Look at it now and do the tasks on page 87.

COMPANY PROFILE	
Company name	Heller AG
Headquarters	Dortmund, Germany
Company activity	Manufacturer of headlights for the automotive industry
Employees	27,000 worldwide in 30 countries
Turnover (annual sales)	5.2 billion EUR (last year)

A 'horseless carriage' around 1900. Hans and Gerda Frohmüller made the first headlights for the very first German cars. Today, the family sells headlights around the world.

Heller AG is one of the world's top 50 companies which manufactures components for the automotive industry. Its headquarters are in Germany, but the company has sales offices and factories around the world and employs 27,000 people. The company was founded in 1901 by a brother and sister, Hans and Gerda Frohmüller, who made lights for the earliest cars in a small factory near their home. Heller is still a family-owned company. Last year, the company earned over 5 billion (5,000,000,000) euros from the sale of its products worldwide.

M, I **A Find the English words and phrases in the profile for these German expressions. Compare your answers with a partner, then report to the class.**

1 Hauptsitz
2 gegründet werden
3 (ein Produkt) herstellen
4 Fabrik
5 Verkaufsbüro
6 Firma in Familienbesitz
7 Umsatz
8 Absatz (eines Produktes)
9 Angestellte/r
10 Tätigkeiten der Firma

Tips and tricks

The word 'headquarters' is **plural**!

The firm's headquarters are in Germany.

Their headquarters ~~is~~ in Germany.

R **B Here are some typical things that you can read about a company in its profile. Match the sentence halves.**

1 The company's headquarters
2 The company was founded
3 Its turnover is
4 It has
5 The company employs

a in 1856.
b around 20,000 people worldwide.
c factories and sales offices in 15 countries.
d are in Detroit, Michigan.
e over $1 billion (a year).

R **C This is Yvonne Kinkel. Yvonne works for Heller in Dortmund. Groups of people often visit the factory there. When they arrive, Yvonne welcomes them and gives a short talk about the company. She is doing that now. Complete what she says with information from the company's profile.**

"Good morning, ladies and gentlemen. Welcome to the Heller factory here in (1) …. My name is Yvonne Kinkler, and this morning I want to tell you first a bit about our company.

OK. Well, the company was found in (2) … . A brother and sister, (3) … and (4) … Frohmüller, started it in (5) … near their home. They made the very first headlights for the first (6) … carriages. We still manufacture headlights today, over a hundred years later. In fact, we are one of the world's (7) …. And we are not just in Germany now. Our headquarters are here, but we have factories and sales offices in (8) … countries around the world. Worldwide, Heller has (9) … employees – that's a lot of people!"

OK. That's a very quick introduction. Let's go now and look at the factory. Could you please put on these hard hats first? They're for you safety …

P, I **D Now YOU! Imagine that you are Yvonne. The class is your group of visitors. Write your own short introduction to Heller – try to make it different to Yvonne's – then welcome the class and give your talk.**

Product catalogues (Unit 4)

This is Dennis Hamann. He works in a factory in Germany. Dennis has to buy some new safety equipment for the factory. He finds a company in the UK that makes good quality equipment at good prices and he gets a catalogue from them. Today, he wants to phone the company and buy some equipment. You can see a page from the catalogue below. Look at it now and do the tasks on page 89.

Good morning. I'm calling from Germany. My name's Hamann. I'd like to order …

	**SAFETY HELMET (HARD HAT)** (Available in blue, green, yellow or white) PRODUCT CODE: EN397	€ 24.50
	**SAFETY GOGGLES** PRODUCT CODE: JS341	€ 12.80
	**SAFETY SPECTACLES** PRODUCT CODE: 3M1044	€ 8.95
	**WELDING FACE SHIELD** Complete protection for face, head and neck PRODUCT CODE: IP0286	€ 61.50
	**EAR PROTECTORS** PRODUCT CODE: EP7149	~~€ 15.00~~ NOW ONLY € 10.50 SPECIAL OFFER
	**WORK BOOTS** PRODUCT CODE BL91654	€ 37.85

P, I **A Practise saying the letters of the English alphabet and prices. Look at the information boxes, then, with a partner, say the letters and prices below out loud.**

You say the letters of the English alphabet like this …					You say prices in English like this …	
A ay	**G** dschee	**L** ell	**Q** kyew	**V** vee	1€	one euro
B bee	**H** aitch	**M** emm	**R** are	**W** double-you	2€	two euro**s** (two ~~euro~~!!)
C see	**I** eye	**N** enn	**S** ess	**X** eks	1.50€	one euro fifty
D dee	**J** dschay	**O** oh	**T** tea	**Y** why	2.75€	two euro**s** seventy-five
E ee	**K** kay	**P** pee	**U** you	**Z** zed	15.25	fifteen euro**s** twenty-five
F eff						

CAT	OLH	DWI	AQV	RTU	ZGY
1.50€	10€	3.75€	6.90€	1.80€	79.95€

R, P, I **B Dennis is on the phone to the company in the UK. Complete his conversation with information from the catalogue on page 88, then read the dialogue aloud with a partner.**

Saleswoman **Dennis**

SafeAtWork Limited. Good morning. How may I help you today?

Good morning. I'm calling from Germany. My name's Hamann. I'd like to order some of your equipment.

Certainly, Mr Hamann. What equipment would you like?

OK. First I'd like to order some safety goggles. The product code is (1) …

How many pairs would you like? They are (2) € … each.

Fifty pairs, please.

OK, I've got that.

Then I'd also like ten pairs of the (3) …

That's product code three M one-oh-four-four?

Right. They're (4) € … each, I think.

Yes, that's right. And you said ten pairs?

Yes, please. And finally, I'd like fifty ear protectors. The product code is (5) ….

They're on special offer at the moment so the price is only (6) € … each.

Great. That's it then, please.

I'll just repeat that, Mr Hamman. You'd like to order (7) …. Is that correct?

Yes, that's absolutely right.

Thanks very much for your order. We'll send the equipment today. The invoice will be with the equipment.

Thanks for your help. Bye now.

Goodbye, Mr Hamann.

P, I **C Now You! With your partner, write and read out another new phone call to SafeAtWork Ltd. Use the catalogue on page 88.**

Writing an advertisement (Unit 5)

Kate is the business manager of Party People in Danbury. Today, she wants to advertise the firm and she is writing an advertisement. It is a 'flyer' – a sheet of paper that she can put up in the windows of shops etc. or give to people in the street. You can see Kate's flyer below. Look at it and do the tasks on page 91.

R, P, I **A** **With a partner, look at the flyer and the notes below. Then use the phrases to explain how Kate's flyer 'works'. Give a short talk to the class.**

1 Your flyer must 'grab attention' ("Look at me!"). A picture is a good way to do this.
2 A 'slogan' is also a good idea. When people think of your firm, they think of your slogan.
3 Now the person who is looking at your flyer must want to read it – be interested. A question is often a good way to do this.
4 In a flyer, you must always speak directly to the person who is looking at it. Use the words 'you' ('your' etc.) as often as you can.
5 After people read your flyer they must *do something* – buy your product or service! They must see *how* they can do this.
6 Finally, remember to tell them the name of your company – at the top and again at the end.

Kate's flyer is for the firm Party people.
First, the flyer must 'grab attention' so Kate has a photo of …
Beneath the picture there is the firm's slogan: "…"
Kate wants people to be interested in her flyer so she begins the text with …
She speaks directly to the readers. For example, …
So how can people contact Party People? Well, Kate …
Of course, Kate tells people the name of her firm. She …

P, I **B** **Now YOU! Work in a small group to make a poster. The poster is a big flyer for a product or service that you can choose yourselves. There are some ideas below to get you started.** → Skills 16

1 In your group, choose a product or service that you want to advertise.
2 Think of a name for your firm and a good slogan.
3 Find a picture.
4 Write your text – don't forget the 'contact details'!
5 Make your poster.
6 Organise a gallery walk in class and show and explain your flyer to the others. You can use the phrases above again.

The Corner Café
Hairdresser
Luigi's Pizzas (Free Delivery!)
Ben's Burger Bar
MOPS Cleaning Service
Bob's Builder's

A business letter (Unit 6)

Nicole Skorikova works for *Der Kleine Regenbogen*, a national chain of children's nurseries in Germany. Today, Nicole has to buy some play equipment for the nurseries. She wants to buy a lot of equipment so she must find the best price. On the internet, Nicole has found a list of companies that make equipment. Some are in Germany, but others are in Britain and other countries. She is writing to all of them. She wants to ask about their equipment, prices, when they can deliver etc. Then she will choose the best company. A letter like this is called an 'enquiry' – in German, 'eine Anfrage'. You can see Nicole's letter to a British firm below. Look at it now and do the tasks on page 93.

Der Kleine Regenbogen GmbH 1

Heinrichstraße 27
40225 Düsseldorf
GERMANY

2 Home of Play Ltd
39-41 Abbey Road
Birmingham
GB-BM12 4CB

3 **Our Ref:** KR/NS1
21 March 20..

4 Dear Sirs

5 **Product enquiry**

We saw information about your play equipment products on your website and would like further information.

We are a chain of over 40 children's nurseries in Germany. You can find more information about us on our website: www.derkleineregenbogen.de.

If your prices and quality are right, we may want to buy a quantity of your products for our nurseries. Please let us know about discounts and your terms of payment. We would also like samples of your products to test for quality and safety.

We look forward to hearing from you soon.

6 Yours sincerely,

Nicole Skorikova

Nicole Skorikova

R, P **A Business letters usually have a standard layout. Here are the most important parts of a letter. Find them in Nicole's letter, then explain her letter to the class.**

1 LETTERHEAD: this gives the firm's name, address etc.
2 INSIDE ADDRESS: the firm/person/people you are writing to.
3 REFERENCE and DATE. The reference often includes the initials of the writer of the letter.
4 When you write for the first time to a company – and don't know people's names – begin 'Dear Sirs'.
5 SUBJECT: why you are writing.
6 CLOSE: 'Yours sincerely' then your signature and name.

Nicole's letter has a letterhead. It gives the ...
The inside address shows that she is writing to ...
Nicole's reference in this letter is .... The date is ...
She begins her letter ... because ...
Her subject is: '...' because ...
She ends her letter with ...

M **B Here are some phrases that are useful in an enquiry. Match the English and German phrases.**

1 We saw information about your products on the internet / in a magazine.
2 We would like further information.
3 We are ... (a big company in Germany / ...)
4 If your prices and quality are right, we may want to buy ...
5 Please let us know about ...
6 discounts
7 your terms of payment
8 We would also like samples of your products to test for quality and safety.
9 We look forward to hearing from you soon.

a Bitte informieren Sie uns über ....
b Rabatte
c Wenn Ihre Preise und Qualität zutreffend sind, würden wir gerne ... kaufen.
d Wir hätte auch gerne Muster Ihrer Produkte, um sie auf Qualität und Sicherheit zu testen.
e Wir freuen uns darauf, bald von Ihnen zu hören.
f Wir sind ... (eine große Firma in Deutschland / ...).
g Ihre Zahlungsbedingungen
h Wir haben im Internet / in einer Zeitschrift Informationen über Ihr Produkt gesehen.
i Wir hätten gerne weitere Informationen.

Wonderful British CAKES, BISCUITS and JAMS!

We make and export the very best English food products – and our prices are amazing! For more information contact us today!
BEST OF BRITISH LTD
17 Earl Grey Street
LONDON N11 5AW

P **C Now YOU! You work for a large shop in your town. You want to buy some British food to sell in your shop and you find this advertisement in a magazine. Write an enquiry letter to the firm.**

TEST

1 Reading

You find the article below online. Read the text and do the tasks on page 95.

Fishing in Alaska is a cold, hard job!

There are many different jobs in America from shop assistants to circus clowns, but what are the most dangerous – which workers have the kinds of jobs where it is possible that they may die? In this article, we look at …

America's most dangerous jobs!

Police officers and firefighters have dangerous jobs. We see them on TV or in movies. Their jobs are famous – maybe even 'exciting'. But, in fact, they aren't the most dangerous jobs in America today.

The number one dangerous job in the USA today is a timber cutter. These people work high in the air with dangerous machines and big trees. Most die or are badly injured when trees fall on them. Every year, per every 100,000 timber workers, 120 die.

The number two most dangerous job is a fisher. Fishing is always dangerous but in the far north of the USA, in Alaska, in winter, it can be a really terrible job. Alaskan fishers catch crabs in winter. They work hundreds of kilometres from land, in storms, ice and snow. The temperature can sometimes be 40 degrees below freezing. And they often work 40 hours in every 50 hours. It is perhaps not surprising, therefore, that around 70 fishers die every year per 100,000 workers.

Another dangerous job is that of a steel worker. You have maybe seen them at work on tall buildings like skyscrapers. Clearly, these people work high in the air every day and there is always the possibility that they can fall. In fact, per 100,000 steel workers, 60 die every year – most because they fall. This really is a job for people who are young and physically very fit.

The big airliners we fly in when we go on holiday are very safe and passengers never die. But every year in the USA, around 70 pilots die in small planes. One of the most dangerous jobs for a pilot is to be a crop sprayer. When they are spraying crops, pilots must fast

America's most dangerous job? A timber cutter.

Some pilots fly small planes like this one. They spray crops to protect them against insects and diseases

< left: A steel worker at work on a **skyscraper**
> right: Around 25 truck drivers per 100,000 die every year on America's highways

and very, very low. They know that if they make one mistake, they will crash and that the crash can kill them.

Finally, the other most dangerous jobs in America are on the roads. Traffic is always dangerous. In New York, cycle couriers deliver thousands of letters and packages every day to offices in the city. They have to work fast and they often hold cars and trucks with their hands so that they can go faster. Lots of them die or have bad accidents. But the most dangerous job on the roads is to be a truck driver. Every year, around 25 per 100,000 die in an accident. Most of the time this happens when drivers work too long hours. They become tired and then they fall asleep on the road. The result is almost always a bad accident or death.

A Decide whether the sentences below are true or false according to the text. Write down T or F.

1 Police officers and firefighters have the most dangerous jobs in the USA.
2 The people who build skyscrapers are called steel workers.
3 Small planes are safe but big airliners are dangerous.
4 Cycle couriers in New York often travel in cars or trucks.
5 Per 100,000 truck drivers, around 25 die every year in accidents.

B Choose the correct answer. Write down a, b or c.

1 Alaskan fishers often work
a high in the air. b very long hours. c in small ships.

2 The reason why truck drivers often have accidents is that they
a fall. b fly too low. c don't stop to rest.

3 New York cycle couriers
a deliver things. b protect people. c always have bad accidents.

4 Most timber cutters die because of
a falling trees. b dangerous machines. c small mistakes when they fly.

5 All of the workers in this text have jobs that
a are exciting. b are easy. d can kill them.

→ per *pro* → crab *Krebs* → physically *körperlich* → courier *Kurier, Eilbote*

2 Listening

A 1.26

You are going to hear a recording of a young British woman called Becky. You will hear the recording twice. Listen and choose the correct answers. Write down a, b, c.

1 Becky is
  a an office worker. b a teacher. c a tour guide.

2 Becky's company has existed since
  a 1906. b 1806. c 1706.

2 Back then people
  a liked coffee better than tea.
  b liked tea better than coffee.
  c didn't drink tea or coffee.

3 Thomas Turner opened his first shop
  a in the building next door to where Becky is now.
  b in the building where Becky is now.
  c in a building in the next street to where Becky is now.

4 Tea was soon 'in' in London because
  a Thomas Turner was a famous man.
  b Thomas Turner's tea was cheap.
  c famous people came to his tea shop.

5 1837 was an important year because
  a Thomas Turner opened a second shop.
  b the British queen at the time started buying Turners tea.
  c the British queen at the time visited Thomas Turner's tea shop.

6 Today, Turners sells its tea in … countries around the world
  a 23 b 32 c 33

7 Becky says it's 'amazing' that
  a Indian people drink Turners tea.
  b Americans drink Turners tea.
  c British people still like Turners tea.

8 The modern Turners company has … employees.
  a 1,200 b 3,200 c 2,300

9 Last year, the company's turnover was
  a around $1 billion.
  b over $1 billion.
  c almost $1 billion.

10 Next, the visitors will go to
  a Turners head office. b a museum. c Turners tea shop.

3 Mediation

A **Du bist mit Freunden im Urlaub in Neuseeland. Deine Freunde sprechen kein Englisch und wollen wissen, was diese Schilder bedeuten. Erkläre sie ihnen kurz auf Deutsch.**

1

2

3

4

B **Now explain to an English person – in English of course – what these German signs at work mean.**

1

2

3

4

4 Writing

You see this advertisement for a work experience placement in the UK. Write an email (80 – 100 words) in which you apply for the placement.

Say:
- where you saw the advertisment
- who you are
- that you attach your CV
- if you have any work experience in Germany (e.g. a part-time job)
- why you would like to get the placement

Begin and end you email in a suitable way.

PRAKTIKE.EU
WORK EXPERIENCE IN THE UK

Are you interested in working for two weeks in a famous British shop in the heart of London? Horrids is offering three work experience placements from 1 – 14 September. The placements will be suitable for full-time college students from the EU. You will not be paid for the work, but we will give you travel expenses in London and a free lunch every day. Please write to us at horrids.co.uk and attach your CV! Hurry! We hope to hear from you soon!

Anhang

Grammar summary
Skills files
Vocabulary

GRAMMAR SUMMARY

1 Das simple present

A Allgemein

Das simple present wird verwendet:
- für Aussagen, die längere Zeit gültig sind,
- um auszudrücken, was jemand regelmäßig tut.

B Mit *sometimes*, *often* usw.

Da man mit dem simple present ausdrückt, was man regelmäßig tut, wird es oft mit Wörtern wie *usually*, *normally*, *sometimes*, *often*, *always*, *never* verwendet. Diese Wörter (Adverbien) stehen immer:
- **vor** einem Vollverb,
- **nach** *to be*.

I **usually** get up at 7 a.m.

I **often** watch TV in the evenings.

I'm **always** happy on Fridays.

C Bildung: Aussagen

Das simple present wird aus der Grundform des Verbs (Infinitiv ohne *to*) gebildet. Nach *he / she / it* endet das Verb immer auf *-s* oder *-es*!

a An die meisten Verben wird einfach *-s* angehängt.
b Die Endung *-es* wird bei Verben benutzt, die auf *s*, *ss*, *x*, *ch*, oder *sh* enden (z. B. *to finish*), da es schwer wäre, nur ein *-s* auszusprechen.
c Auch *to go* und *to do* enden mit *-es*.
d Ein Sonderfall sind Verben, die auf *-y* enden: *to tidy* ⟶ *he tid**ies***.

a to work	b to finish
I work he / she / it work**s** we work you work they work	I finish he / she / it finish**es** we finish you finish they finish

c to go	d to tidy
I go he / she / it go**es** we go you go they go	I tidy he / she / it tid**ies** we tidy you tidy they tidy

D Bildung: Fragen und Verneinungen

- Fragen im simple present werden mit *do* (bei *he / she / it*: *does*) gebildet.
- Verneinungen bildet man mit *don't* (nach *he / she / it*: *doesn't*).

VORSICHT!
Nach *does / doesn't* kommt immer die Grundform des Verbs:
*Does he work? (**!** Does he ~~works~~?)*
*She doesn't work. (**!** She doesn't ~~works~~.)*

Fragen	Verneinungen
Do I work? **Does** he / she / it work? Do we work? Do you work? Do they work?	I don't work he / she / it **doesn't** work we don't work you don't work they don't work

2 Das present continuous

A Allgemein

Das present continuous benutzt man für Aktivitäten, die gerade im Augenblick des Sprechens stattfinden. Oder auch um ein Bild zu beschreiben. Es wird häufig mit Zeitangaben wie *at the moment* und *right now* verwendet.

I'**m reading** this text at the moment.

What can you see in this photo?
– A hairdresser. Right now, she'**s cutting** a customer's hair.

B Mit *this week, this month* usw.

Das present continuous kann auch für längere, befristete Handlungen verwendet werden, die gerade stattfinden, benutzt werden, z. B. *this week, this month.*

We'**re visiting** some friends in England this week.
Julia **is learning** English on a course in London.

C Bildung: Aussagen

Das present continuous wird mit *to be* und Verb + *-ing* gebildet.

I'm he's / she's / it's we're you're they're	working	I'm not working she isn't working
		Am I working? Are you working? Are they working?

D Bildung: Fragen und Verneinungen

Fragen und Verneinungen werden mit den Frage- und Verneinungsformen von *to be* gebildet.

Verb + *-ing*: Schreibregeln

- An die meisten Verben wird einfach *-ing* angehängt: *work – work**ing**, do – do**ing**.*
- Verben, die auf *-e* enden, verlieren das *-e*: *us**e** – us**ing**, danc**e** – danc**ing**.*
- Kurze Verben, die auf einen Vokal und einen Konsonanten (außer *-y, -w* und *-x)* enden, verdoppeln den Konsonanten: *cu**t** – cu**tt**ing* (aber *pla**y** – pla**y**ing*).
- Längere Verben, die auf einen Vokal und einen Konsonanten enden, verdoppeln den Konsonanten nicht: *visi**t** – visi**t**ing, delive**r** – delive**r**ing.* (Ausnahmen: *trave**ll**ing, begi**nn**ing*)
- Bei Verben, die auf *-ie* enden, wird *-ie* zu *-y*: ***die** – **dy**ing*

This is Patrick. He lives in England. He goes to an FE college five days a week.

It's 8.30 in the morning. Patrick is going to college by bus.

3 Das simple past

A Allgemein

Das simple past wird verwendet, um Ereignisse in der Vergangenheit zu schildern, die jetzt abgeschlossen sind. Es wird häufig mit Zeitangaben wie *then*, *in 1970*, *last week* und *30 years ago* benutzt.

B Bildung: Aussagen

- Regelmäßige Verben bilden das simple past mit *-ed*. Diese Form bleibt in allen Personen gleich.
- Unregelmäßige Verben haben Sonderformen im simple past (eine Liste findest du auf dem Klappumschlag). Diese Formen (außer bei *to be*) bleiben ebenfalls in allen Personen gleich.

regelmäßig	unregelmäßig	
to work	**to go**	**to be**
I worked	I went	I **was**
he worked	he went	he was
she worked	she went	she was
it worked	it went	it was
we worked	we went	we **were**
you worked	you went	you were
they worked	they went	they were

C Bildung: Fragen und Verneinungen

- Fragen im simple past werden in allen Personen mit *did* gebildet.
- Verneinungen bildet man durchgehend mit *didn't*.
- *to be* bildet Fragen und Verneinungen im simple past mit eigenen Formen.

Fragen	Verneinungen
Did I work?	I didn't work
Did he / she / it work?	he / she / it didn't work
Did we work?	we didn't work
Did you work?	you didn't work
Did they work?	they didn't work

to be	
Was I?	I wasn't
Was he / she / it?	he / she / it wasn't
Were we / you / they?	we / you / they / weren't

VORSICHT!
Nach *did / didn't* steht immer die Grundform des Verbs:
Did he work? (! Did he ~~worked~~?)
She didn't work. (! She didn't ~~worked~~.)

Verb + *-ed*: Schreibregeln
- An die meisten Verben wird einfach *-ed* angehängt: *work – work**ed***.
- An Verben, die auf *-e* enden, hängt man nur *-d* an: *us**e** – use**d**, danc**e** – dance**d***.
- Kurze Verben, die auf einen Vokal *(a, e, i o, u)* und einen Konsonanten (außer *-y*, *-w* und *-x*) enden, verdoppeln den Konsonanten: *sho**p** – shop**ped**, jo**g** – jog**ged***.
- Längere Verben, die auf einen Vokal und einen Konsonanten enden, verdoppeln den Konsonanten nicht:
  *visi**t** – visit**ed**, delive**r** – deliver**ed***. (Ausnahme: *travel**led***)
- Bei Verben, die auf *-y* enden, wird *-y* zu *-i*: *stud**y** – stud**ied***.

4 Das present perfect

A Allgemein

Mit dem present perfect und *since / for* kann man 'Wie lange'-Fragen *(How long …?)* beantworten.

- *Since* wird mit einem Zeitpunkt (z. B. *2001, 3 January, last year*) benutzt.
- *For* verwendet man für einen Zeitraum (z. B. *two years, six months*).

B Bildung: Aussagen

Das present perfect wird mit *to have* und der 3. Form (Partizip Perfekt) gebildet.

- Regelmäßige Verben (wie *to work*) bilden ihre 3. Form mit *-ed*.
- Unregelmäßige Verben (wie *to go*) haben Sonderformen, die in der Liste auf dem Klappumschlag zu finden sind.

I have (I've) he has (he's) she has (she's) it has (it's) we have (we've) you have (you've) they have (they've)	worked gone

C Bildung: Fragen und Verneinungen

Fragen und Verneinungen werden mit Frage- und Verneinungsformen von *to have* + 3. Form des Verbs gebildet.

Have you worked? Has he worked?
I haven't worked he / she / it hasn't worked we / you / they haven't worked

5 Das past perfect

A Allgemein

Das past perfect wird für ein Ereignis in der Vergangenheit verwendet, das noch vor einem zweiten Ereignis in der Vergangenheit stattfand. Für das länger zurückliegende Ereignis verwendet man das past perfect, für das nicht ganz so lange zurückliegende das simple past. Wir verwenden das past perfect häufig mit *after*.

She **chose** her job after she **had visited** an interesting company.

B Bildung

Das past perfect wird mit *had* + 3. Form (Partizip Perfekt) des Verbs gebildet. Fragen werden auch mit *had*, Verneinungen mit *hadn't* gebildet.

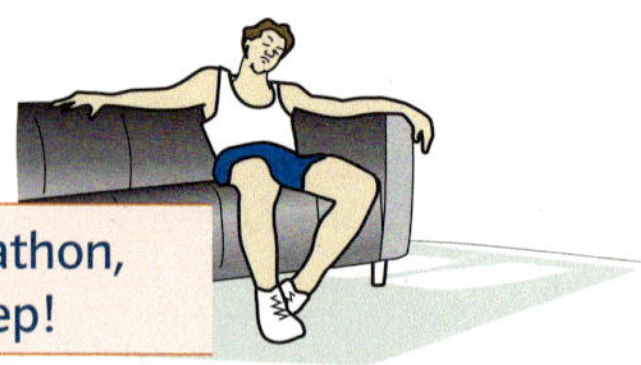

After Jamie had run in the marathon, he went home and went to sleep!

Aussagen	Verneinungen
I had worked he / she / it had worked we / you / they had worked	I hadn't worked he / she / it hadn't worked we / you / they hadn't worked

Fragen
Had I worked? Had he / she / it worked? Had we / you / they worked?

6. Das Futur: *will*

A Allgemein

Will wird für feststehende Ereignisse in der Zukunft sowie für Vorhersagen und Vermutungen verwendet.

I'**ll have** a family in 10 years.
She **won't leave** her job when she has a family.

B Bildung

- **Aussagen** werden mit *will* + Grundform des Verbs gebildet. Die Kurzform (*'ll*) wird fast immer beim Sprechen und häufig auch beim Schreiben verwendet.
- **Fragen** bildet man, indem man *will* und das Subjekt tauscht. Hier sind die Kurzformen nicht möglich.
- **Verneinungen** werden mit *won't* + Grundform des Verbs gebildet.

I will (I'll) come	Will I come?
he will (he'll) come	Will he come?
she will (she'll) come	Will she come?
it will (it'll) come	Will it come?
we will (we'll) come	Will we come?
you will (you'll) come	Will you come?
they will (they'll) come	Will they come?
I won't come he / she / it won't come we / you / they won't come	

7. Das Futur: *going to*

A Allgemein

Going to verwendet man, um über Pläne und Vorhaben zu sprechen: *I'm going to buy a new jacket* entspricht etwa auf Deutsch: „Ich habe vor, eine neue Jacke zu kaufen."

I'm going to move to a new apartment next month.
Are you **going to** leave home?

B Bildung

- **Aussagen** bildet man mit *to be* + *going to* + Hauptverb.
- **Fragen** bildet man mit den Frageformen von *to be* + *going to* + Hauptverb.
- Für **Verneinungen** benutzt man die Verneinung von *to be* + *going to* + Hauptverb.

I'm he's / she's / it's we're / you're / they're	going to	work
Am I Is he / she / it Are we / you / they	going to	work?
I'm not he / she / it isn't we / you / they aren't	going to	work

Will* und *going to

8 Modale Hilfsverben: *must, have to, mustn't* und *don't / doesn't have to*

A Allgemein

Mit den modalen Hilfsverben *must, have to, mustn't* und *don't / doesn't have to* wird ausgedrückt, was man tun muss, nicht tun darf und nicht zu tun braucht (nicht tun muss).

- **must / have to**
  In England you must / have to drive on the left.

- **mustn't**
  You mustn't drive on the right!

- **don't / doesn't have to**
  He doesn't have to drive! He has a driver.

Must und *have to* haben etwa die gleiche Bedeutung. Sie drücken aus, was man tun **muss**.	*Mustn't* drückt aus, was man **nicht darf**. **VORSICHT!** *mustn't* bedeutet **nicht** ‚nicht müssen'.	*Don't / Doesn't have to* drückt aus, was man **nicht zu tun braucht**. **VORSICHT!** *don't have to* = nicht müssen

B Bildung: *must* und *have to*

- *Must* bleibt in allen Personen gleich. Auf *must* folgt die Grundform des Verbs.
- *Have to* bildet man mit *to have* + Grundform des Verbs.

must	have to
I must go he / she / it must go we / you / they must go	I have to go he / she / it has to go we / you / they have to go

C Bildung: *mustn't*

Mustn't bleibt ebenfalls bei allen Personen gleich. Auf *mustn't* folgt die Grundform des Verbs.

I mustn't he / she / it mustn't we / you / they mustn't	go

D Bildung: *don't / doesn't have to*

Die Verneinungsform von *have to* bildet man mit *don't / doesn't have to* + Grundform des Verbs.

I don't have to he / she / it doesn't have to we / you / they don't have to	go

9 *If*-Sätze (Bedingungssätze)

A Allgemein

- Ein Bedingungssatz besteht aus einem *if*-Teil und einem Hauptsatz. Der *if*-Teil beschreibt eine Bedingung und der Hauptsatz drückt aus, was passieren wird oder passieren könnte (oder hätte passieren können), wenn diese Bedingung erfüllt wird.
- Bedingungssätze können entweder mit dem *if*-Teil oder mit dem Hauptsatz beginnen. Wenn der *if*-Teil beginnt, steht immer ein Komma vor dem Hauptsatz.
- Es gibt drei Grundtypen von *if*-Sätzen: Typ 1, 2 und 3.

B *If*-Sätze Typ 1:

***If** you **ask** the robot, it **will clean** the house.*
- Typ 1 drückt aus, was unter bestimmten Bedingungen in der Zukunft geschehen wird oder nicht geschehen wird.

If + simple present	will + Verb
If you go to the party,	you'll see Mitch.

C *If*-Sätze Typ 2:

***If** I **worked** for that company, I **would need** a good qualification.*
- Wir benutzen Typ 2, um über eventuelle Situationen zu sprechen oder wenn du zweifelst, dass eine Bedingung erfüllbar ist.
- **VORSICHT!** Anders als im Deutschen darf *would* nur im Hauptsatz, nicht im *if*-Teil stehen.

If + simple past	would(n't) + Verb
If you went to the party,	you would see Mitch.

D *If*-Sätze Typ 3:

***If** he **had stayed** on the streets, he **would have died**.*
- Typ 3 schildert Ereignisse in der Vergangenheit, die hätten passieren können – die aber nicht passiert sind.

If + past perfect	would(n't) have + Partizip Perfekt (3. Form)
If you had gone to the party,	you would have seen Mitch.

Typ 1: Für Sachen, die passieren werden, wenn …

Typ 2: Für imaginäre, schwer vorstellbare Situationen

Typ 3: Für Sachen, die hätten passieren können

10 Das Passiv

A Allgemein: Aktiv- und Passivsätze

- Aktivsätze betonen, **wer** etwas tut. Passivsätze betonen, **was** getan wird – die Handlung steht im Vordergrund.
- In *Kickoff Foundation* findest du nur **Aktivsätze**. In einem Aktivsatz steht das Subjekt vor dem Verb. Gibt es ein Objekt, so steht dieses nach dem Verb.
- **Passivsätze** kann man als ‚umgedrehte' Aktivsätze ansehen: Das Objekt des Aktivsatzes wird zum Subjekt des Passivsatzes.

Aktivsatz

Subjekt	Verb	Objekt
The man	bought	the flowers.

Passivsatz

The man	*bought*	***the flowers.***
The flowers	*were bought*	***by the man.***

B Bildung

- Das Passiv wird mit *to be* + 3. Form des Verbs (Partizip Perfekt) gebildet.

simple present		simple past	
I'm he's she's it's we're you're they're	**made**	I was he was she was it was we were you were they were	**made**

C Mit oder ohne *by*?

Meist wird das Subjekt des Aktivsatzes in einem Passivsatz nicht genannt. Wollen wir aber das Subjekt besonders betonen, können wir es mit Hilfe von *by* am Satzende anfügen. In Satz **a** ist der Name des Regisseurs besonders wichtig. In Satz **b** ist es uninteressant, von wem die Blumen angebaut werden.

a *The film was made* ***by Steven Spielberg****.*
b *These flowers are grown in* ***Kenya*** *(by …).*

They delivered oranges to the supermarket yesterday.

Too many oranges were delivered to the supermarket yesterday!

11 Adjektive und Adverbien

A Allgemein

- **Adjektive** beschreiben Personen und Sachen. Sie stehen meist vor einem Substantiv oder nach *to be*.
- **Adverbien** sagen etwas über Verben aus. Sie sagen uns, **wie** etwas passiert

a **big** robot
The robot is **big**.

The robot loads the lorries **quickly**.

B Adverbien: Bildung

- Ein Adverb wird gebildet, indem *-ly* an das Adjektiv angehängt wird.
- Bei Adjektiven mit der Endung *-y* wird das *-y* zu *-ily*.
- Die Endung *-le* wird zu *-ly*.
- *-ic* wird zu *-ically*.
- Das Adverb von *good* ist *well*.

Adjektiv	Adverb
quick	quick**ly**
easy	eas**ily**
simple	simp**ly**
automatic	automat**ically**
good	**well**

12 Relativsätze

A Allgemein

Relativsätze sind Sätze, die eines der Relativpronomen *who*, *which* oder *where* enthalten. Sie beschreiben das Wort, auf das sie sich beziehen, näher.

The woman who is helping him is Frau Bliscz.
The document which she has in her hand is Herr Krueger's boarding card.

D *who*, *which* oder *where*?

- *who* für Personen
- *which* für Sachen
- *where* für Orte

A passenger is a person **who** travels by plane.
A plane is a machine **which** carries people.
The place **where** passengers check in is the check-in desk.

Boris can do things very quickly.

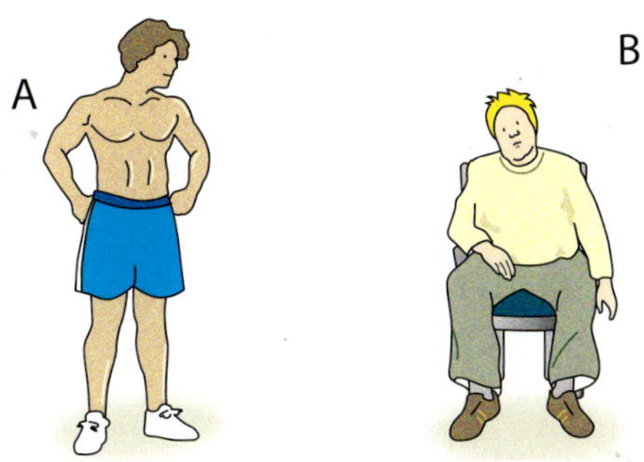

The guy who goes to a fitness club every day is A or B?

SKILLS FILES

1 Einen längeren Text verstehen

Vor dem Lesen:

1. Woher kommt der Text: Zeitung? Sachbuch? Roman? … ?
2. Handelt es sich um einen Sachtext oder um einen fiktionalen Text?
3. Was erwartest du, wenn du die Bilder und den Titel ansiehst? Wird der Text sachlich, spannend, informativ, … sein?
4. Weißt du etwas über den Autor und die Zeit, in der der Text spielt bzw. geschrieben wurde?

Beim ersten Lesen:

Lies den Text. Ist er so, wie du erwartet hast? Was ist anders?

Beim zweiten Lesen:

Wie kannst du die Bedeutung der neuen Wörter erschließen?

A crazy idea!

For centuries stories about UFOs and aliens have attracted people: Spaceships land on the Earth, people go out to take photos and never **return**, aliens enter the **brains** of people and control their bodies, **hideous** creatures try to **take control of** our world. Many people all over the world believe that there are aliens on the Earth. There are thousands of stories from people who **claim** that they have seen UFOs, met aliens or been on an alien planet. But **astronomers** and other scientists are more **sceptical**. They want facts not fiction. They say that the chances of meeting an alien are not very high and most of these stories come from people who have **visions**. Others have a lot of **imagination** and believe that what they imagined really happened.

Schau dir die markierten Wörter an und lies dazu folgende Tipps:

Vergleich: Was könnte das englische Wort *return* bedeuten? Überlege, ob du ein ähnliches Wort in einer anderen Sprache kennst: z.B das französische Wort *retourner*.
Logische Ableitung: Das Wort *body* ist dir bekannt. Was könnte dann *brain* sein, wenn es deinen Körper kontrolliert?
Kontext: Ein Wort wie *hideous* kannst du nur mithilfe der Wörter erraten, die es umgeben. Ist es wohl eher ein positives Wort wie *beautiful* oder ein negatives wie *horrible*?
Wortbildung: Du kennst bereits das Nomen *control*. Was könnte der Ausdruck *take control of* bedeuten? Das Verb *imagine* ist dir auch bekannt, so dass *imagination* leicht zu verstehen ist.
Deutsch: Die fehlenden drei neuen Wörter kannst du erraten, weil sie deutschen Wörtern ähneln: z.B.: *sceptical* = skeptisch.
Das heißt, du müsstest nur das Wort *claim* im Wörterbuch nachschlagen, falls du es doch nicht aus dem Kontext heraus verstehen kannst.

Nach dem zweiten Lesen:

1. Was ist das Hauptthema: Astronomers? The Earth? Aliens?
2. Wie ist die Argumentationskette bzw. der Handlungsverlauf: Welches sind die Argumente dafür und dagegen?/Was passiert?
3. Was ist die Schlussfolgerung?/Wie endet der Text?

2 Lesetexte unterscheiden

1. Man kann Texte in zwei Hauptgruppen aufteilen: Sachtexte und fiktionale Texte.

Sachtexte / Nicht fiktionale Texte *(fact)*	Fiktionale Texte *(fiction)*
Anzeige, Zeitungsartikel, Bewerbungsbrief, Biocard, CV (Lebenslauf) usw.	Kurzgeschichte, Auszug aus einem Roman, Erzählung, Gedicht, Lied, Drama usw.

2. Die Texte in diesen Gruppen haben viele Gemeinsamkeiten, aber manches ist doch anders. Hier ein kurzer Überblick. Unten findest du zwei Beispiele. Vielleicht fallen dir noch Punkte ein.

	Eigenschaften	Sachtext	Fiktionaler Text
1	Titel	direkt und informativ	oft indirekt bzw. Wortspiel
2	Bild(er)	Diagramme, Fotos mit klaren Aussagen	Zeichnungen, Stimmungsbilder
3	Anfang	leitet das Thema ein	führt in den Handlungsrahmen ein
4	Absätze	Es wird jeweils ein neuer Sachaspekt eingeleitet bzw. vertieft.	Es wird ein Wechsel von Ort, Zeit, Personen und Handlung angezeigt.
5	Schluss	Schlussfolgerung	sehr unterschiedlich, z. B. Lösung, offenes Ende
6	Ziel des Lesens	Argumente / Infos zur Weiterbearbeitung vermitteln	Unterhaltung, Kritik äußern, Lebenserfahrungen vermitteln
7	Stil	berichtende, zumeist sachliche Sprache	erzählend, oft mit wörtlicher Rede, Fragen, Ausrufen

TAVISTOCK TIMES

(1) UFO reported – 15-year-old missing

(2)

A 15-year-old boy is missing after he went to investigate a UFO on Friday. **(3)** His parents contacted the police the next morning. They reported that their son, Darly, had not come home after he had gone out to take photos of a UFO.

(4) The pupil from a school in Tavistock was last seen on Friday night with two friends after supper. One of them phoned Darly at around 6 o'clock and said that he had seen a UFO over the moors.

(5) The three boys set off on their bikes but only two of them came home at ten o'clock. The parents are certain that their son has been taken by aliens. **(6)** + **(7)**

A **(1)** Sci-Fi adventure story: **(2)**

How we lost Darly

I knew when I phoned Darly that night that he would go with us to the moor. **(3)**

(4) "Of course I'll come with you. I'll get my camera and meet you in ten minutes at the end of the road."

Around 7 o'clock we reached the place where we thought that the UFO had landed. It was dark and windy. Then the rain started. It got so heavy that we decided to wait under a big tree. As we were running to it, Darly fell. He got up again and followed us to the tree.

But then he shouted, "I've dropped my camera!" He went back to look for it but he didn't return.

(5) We searched for an hour but we couldn't find him.

That was the last time we ever saw him. **(6)** + **(7)**

3 Einen englischen Text zusammenfassen

Wenn du eine Geschichte nacherzählst oder Informationen aus einem Text weitergibst, musst du den Inhalt immer kürzen. Dabei darfst du weder etwas Wichtiges vergessen, noch etwas Unwichtiges beibehalten. Diese Tipps können dir helfen, Informationen zu sammeln bzw. eine gute Zusammenfassung zu schreiben.

	Tipps	**Fiktional**	**Nicht fiktional**
1	Copy the text so that you can write on it or mark it.	Stelle sicher, dass du genügend Platz am Rand hast und dass der Zeilenabstand groß genug ist, um zwischen die Zeilen zu schreiben.	
2	Decide how you want to mark the text.	Du kannst Textmarker verwenden oder Bemerkungen an den Rand schreiben. Oft hilft es, verschiedene Farben für verschiedene Punkte einzusetzen.	
3	Read the text again.	Markiere wichtige Dinge / Stellen: z.B. Wörter, Sinnabschnitte und Textteile, Charakterzüge, Atmosphäre, spannende Sätze, …	Markiere wichtige Dinge / Stellen: z.B. Zahlen, Haupt- und Nebenthemen, Argumente oder Namen, die dir wichtig erschei-nen, …
4	Ask questions as you read. (Who? Where? What? When? Why? How?)	Wer sind die Charaktere? Wo befinden sie sich? Was machen sie? Was passiert? Wann passiert es? Warum passiert es? Wie endet die Geschichte?	Welche Infos gibt es zu dem Thema? Welche Argumente werden aufgeführt? Was ist die Schlussfolgerung?
5	Write a rough draft.	Benutze deine eigenen Worte. Wähle einfache Vokabeln und Sätze. Sei sachlich. Füge nicht deine eigene Meinung oder die anderer ein.	
6	Mention only what is important.	Zusammenfassungen sind immer kürzer als der Text. Um eine Kürzung zu erreichen, sollst du Unwichtiges weglassen. Nenne z.B. keine Beispiele, Ausschmückungen, Zitate oder direkte Rede. Verwende auch sprachliche Kürzungen, z.B. das Zusammenziehen von Begriffen zu einer Sachgruppe (*milk, butter, bread* = *food*).	
7	Write a summary or a report.	Verwende das *simple present*.	Verwende die Zeit, in der der Text geschrieben wurde.

4 Texte verfassen

Anbei findest du acht Schritte *(steps)*, die dir helfen können einen guten Text zu schreiben.

1 Task	Was genau ist deine Aufgabe? Was für einen Text sollst du schreiben? Wozu? Worüber?
2 Content	Welche Punkte musst du erwähnen?
3 Type of text	Welche Merkmale hat ein solcher Text?
4 Plan	Mache einen Entwurf. Vergewissere dich, dass du keine Punkte vergessen hast.
5 Words and phrases	Welche *key words* gibt es zu dem Thema? Benutze ein Wörterbuch, falls du Hilfe brauchst. Fallen dir sogar schon ganze Sätze ein? Sammle alle Wörter, Halbsätze und Sätze in einer *mind map*.
6 First copy	Schreibe einen ersten Entwurf. Lass zwischen den Zeilen Platz frei, damit du Korrekturen einfügen kannst.
7 Partner check	Bitte einen Partner / eine Partnerin, deinen Text zu lesen. Versteht er / sie ihn? Baue seine / ihre Korrekturen in deinen Text mit ein.
8 Final copy	Schreibe den Text neu.

VORSICHT! Es gibt viele *false friends* und Fallen im Englischen. Das heißt, dass es manche gleich aussehende Wörter im Englischen und Deutschen gibt, die in den beiden Sprachen aber etwas anderes bedeuten. Hier sind ein paar Beispiele:

German	English	German	English
Handy	mobile (phone)	praktisch	handy
Gymnasium	grammar school	Turnhalle	gym(nasium)
Technik	technology	Methode	technique
Chips	crisps	Pommes frites	chips
Mappe	folder	Karte	map

The end of a beautiful friendship?

5 Eine Postkarte schreiben

Zwischen einer Postkarte aus dem englischsprachigen Ausland und einer Postkarte, wie du sie schreiben würdest, gibt es einige Unterschiede – und nicht nur sprachliche.

1	Greeting	*Hi*, oder *Hello*, mit Namen sind üblich. Du kannst auch *Dear ...*, sagen. Vergiss das Komma nach dem Namen nicht.
2	Date and place	Im *British English* schreibt man oft Datum und Ortsnamen oben rechts vom Text.
3	First word	Das erste Wort wird groß geschrieben.
4	About you	Sage, wie es dir geht und was du gerade tust. *(present continuous)*
5	The weather	Ein oder zwei kurze Sätze genügen.
6	A report	Sage, was du an welchem Tag gemacht hast. (*simple past*)
7	Future plans	Sage, was du vorhast *(want to, will, would like to, ...)* und wann.
8	Short forms	Es wird oft abgekürzt z. B. (*C U ...*, *Luv*)
9	Closing	Vergiss deinen Namen nicht. (*X* = ein Kuss, *O* = eine Umarmung)
10	The name	Anreden wie *Mr*, *Ms* oder *Mrs* brauchst du nicht in der Adresse.
11	The address	Schreibe die Adresse genauso auf, wie du sie von deinem Freund / deiner Freundin bekommen hast.
12	Postcode	Vergiss die Postleitzahl nicht. Sie steht **nach** dem Ort.
13	Country	Wenn du aus dem Ausland schreibst, gib das Zielland an.

6th August, Dublin **(2)**

Hi, Henry, **(1)**
(3) Just to say we are all well and we're having **(4)** a cool time in Ireland. The weather is great! It has been sunny since we arrived. **(5)** Yesterday we spent **(6)** the day in the zoo. Tomorrow **(7)** we want to go to the coast. We hope we can swim there. Hope **(8)** all is well with you and the family. See you **(8)** when we get back to Glasgow.

(8) Luv Fiona. XOX **(9)**

Henry McFarlane **(10)**
209 Westwind Street **(11)**
Glasgow
GL7 6YT **(12)**
Scotland **(13)**

6 Eine Bewerbung schreiben

Wenn du dich auf Englisch um eine Stelle bewirbst, solltest du neben einem Begleitbrief einen Lebenslauf (*CV*) und Kopien sämtlicher Zeugnisse mitschicken. Im Begleitbrief zeigst du, wie gut du schreiben und berichten kannst. Manchmal wird in der Anzeige ein handschriftlich geschriebener Brief verlangt. Übe, bevor du den Brief endgültig abschickst. Den Musterbrief unten kannst du als Vorlage verwenden.

Suzie Tan **(1)**
239 Gordon Ave. **(2)**
Liverpool LI 56 7TU **(3)**

Mr Richard Rich
Sunshine Film Studios
440 Brighton Road
London SW 6 9OP **(3)**

23 July 2012
Ref: Hol2397 **(5)**

Dear Mr Rich **(4)**

(6) With reference to your ad on the Internet on 20th July, I would like to apply for a job as a studio assistant at Sunshine Film Studios in London.
I finished school on June 26. At the moment I am working as an assistant for a photographer. It is a temporary position and I am looking for a permanent job. I would really like to work in London.
I looked at your company's homepage and some of your projects look very interesting. I have some experience of the film world. I had a holiday job in a TV studio last year. My special skills are organizing and working with people.
As you will see from my CV, I was born in China but I speak and write good English and German.
I have some knowledge of Chinese, too. This could be useful with visitors who do not speak English.
I look forward to hearing from you soon.

Yours sincerely **(7)**
Suzie Tan

Encl. **(8)**

1	Name	In englischsprachigen Ländern schreibt man auch zuerst den Vornamen und dann den Nachnamen.
2	Address	Bei Adressen steht die Hausnummer vor dem Straßennamen. Abkürzungen wie *St.* (*Street*) , *Ave.* (*Avenue*), *Cl.* (*Close*), *Pde.* (*Parade*) sind üblich.
3	Postal codes	... sind unterschiedlich in verschiedenen Ländern. Falls du an eine Firma schreibst, schreibe die Adresse genau so, wie sie in der Anzeige steht.
4	Dear ...,	Schreibe *Sir or Madam*, wenn du den Namen der Person nicht kennst. Bei Männernamen schreibe *Mr*, bei Frauennamen *Ms*.
5	Ref:	... bedeutet *reference* oder Betreff.
6	The first word	... schreibt man immer groß.
7	Closing	Wenn du die Anrede *Sir or Madam* verwendest, dann schreibst du *Yours faithfully*. Ansonsten *Yours sincerely*. Vergiss das ‚*s*' bei *Yours* nicht.
8	Encl.	= *enclosed* verwendest du, wenn du weitere Unterlagen beilegst (= Anlagen).

7 Einen Lebenslauf (CV) auf Englisch schreiben

Auf S. 74 siehst du einen teilweise ausgefüllten, englischen Lebenslauf (*CV*). **VORSICHT!** Es ist im englischsprachigen Raum nicht üblich, ein Foto mitzuschicken. Hier sind die wichtigsten Angaben:

1	Name	Vorname, dann Nachname
2	Address	mit Postleitzahl und Land
3	Tel.	mit internationaler Vorwahl
4	Email	Prüfe, ob du sie richtig geschrieben hast!
5	Date of birth	*British English* = Tag / Monat / Jahr *American English* = Monat / Tag / Jahr
6	Place of birth	Stadt + Land
7	Primary school	Voller Name und Adresse + Angabe der Jahreszahlen von … bis …
8	Secondary school	Voller Name und Adresse + Angabe der Jahreszahlen von … bis …
9	Examinations	Name und Datum der Prüfungen
10	Skills	Fähigkeiten und Fertigkeiten, die für den Job wichtig sind z. B.: *computer, photography*
11	Work experience	Praktika und Jobs, die du gemacht hast: Wo? Was? Wann?
12	Interests	Hobbys, Sport, ehrenamtliche Tätigkeiten usw.
13	Referees	Lehrer, Trainer, Arbeitgeber, … (Name, Adresse, Telefonnummer)

CV

CV (curriculum vitae) ist ein lateinischer Begriff und heißt übersetzt „course of life“ (= Lebenslauf).

Referees

Falls der Arbeitgeber sich für dich interessiert, wird er sich mit deinen *referees* in Verbindung setzen. Du benötigst für deinen Arbeitgeber möglicherweise 2–3 Empfehlungsschreiben von *referees*. Sie sollten den Arbeitgeber über deine Persönlichkeit und deine Leistungen im Job informieren. (Bei Bewerbungen im englischsprachigen Raum bekommst du deine Empfehlungsbriefe nicht zu sehen.)

8 Eine formelle E-Mail schreiben

Wie bei einem formellen Brief, schreibst du in einer formellen E-Mail eine Anrede, eine Einleitung und ein paar abschließende Worte.

Der Betreff (*Re*) sagt, worum es geht.	*Re:*
Wenn du den Namen der angesprochenen Person nicht kennst, verwende die Form in Klammern.	*Dear (Sir or Madam) Mr / Ms …,*
Das erste Wort wird groß geschrieben.	*With reference to your …*
Sei immer höflich, auch wenn du dich beschweren willst.	*Would it be possible to … ?* *I'd be very grateful if you could …* *I look forward to hearing from you.*
Verwende die richtige Schlussformel.	*Yours faithfully / sincerely* …

9 Sich auf ein Vorstellungsgespräch vorbereiten

Es ist sehr wichtig, sich auf das Gespräch gut vorzubereiten. Dann kannst du dich während des Vorstellungsgesprächs besser auf das Wesentliche konzentrieren.

Before the interview	1. Informiere dich über die Stelle / das Land / die Firma / … 2. Überlege dir 2–3 Fragen, die du stellen kannst. 3. Mach dir Gedanken, was du zu dem Vorstellungsgespräch anziehst: einen Anzug / Rock / eine Jeans? Deine Kleidung muss auf jeden Fall sauber und gepflegt sein. Trage nicht zu viel Schmuck / Make-up. 4. Bereite dich darauf vor, Fragen des Interviewers zu beantworten.
During the interview	1. Versuche dich zu entspannen. Schau den Interviewer an und lächle! Gib ihm / ihr die Hand, wenn er / sie es möchte. Deine ersten Worte sind wichtig. 2. Achte darauf, wie der Interviewer mit dir redet: Formell? Freundlich? 3. Mach dir keine Sorgen, wenn du nicht alles verstehst. Der Interviewer weiß, dass dein Englisch nicht perfekt ist. Sei ehrlich!

You can ask on the phone	*What do I need to bring with me?* *(Do you pay travel costs?)*	
The interviewer could say	Formal: *Good morning / afternoon / …, Mr / Ms …* *Nice to meet you.* *Please take a seat / sit down, Mr / Ms …*	Informal: *Hi / Hello, Pete / Sue / … !* *Take a seat!*
The interviewer could ask	*Why are you interested in this job?* *Have you worked abroad before?* *What are your best subjects?* *What would you do if you had a difficult customer? / …* *Do you have any questions?*	
If you don't understand something, you can ask	*Could you repeat the question, please?* *Excuse me. Could you say that again, please?* *Excuse me. What does (the word) … mean?* *I'm sorry. Could you speak more slowly, please?*	
You can ask at the interview	*How big is your company?* *How many people work here?*	

Hörtexte verstehen

Vor dem Hören:
Es hilft dir, folgende Punkte zu klären, bevor du versuchst, einen Hörtext zu verstehen:

1. Kontext: Wo kommt der Text her? Was weißt du schon über solche Texte?

Medien			Öffentliche Ansagen			Persönliche Gespräche im Alltag		
Radio	TV	…	Bahnhof	Flughafen	…	live	Telefon	…
Hörspiel, Interview, Film			Z. B. Ansage			Anruf, Gespräch, …		
Oft handelt es sich um einen Bericht oder ein Interview.			Die gesuchte Info kann mit einem Schlüsselwort herausgehört werden. Der Rest ist unwichtig.			Du kannst immer nachfragen, wenn du etwas nicht verstanden hast.		

2. Vorwissen: Was kann dir sonst noch beim Erschließen helfen?

Der Titel	Ein Bild	Die Einführung	Sonstige Kenntnisse
… kann bei einem Film oder einer Sendung hilfreich sein.	… hilft oft dabei, sich ein Bild vom Sprecher bzw. von einer anderen Person / Personen zu machen.	… gibt Hintergrund-informationen bzw. erklärt die Situation.	Wie ist die Person, mit der du redest? Wie könnte sie reagieren?

3. Was möchtest du von dem Text erfahren? (Wer? Wann? Was? Wie? Wo? Warum?)

Allgemeines	Bestimmte Details	Eine Information
Was ist das Hauptthema? Um welches Problem / welchen Inhalt geht es?	Wer redet? Welche Angaben werden zu einem Problem / Thema gemacht?	Detaillierte Angaben zu einer bestimmten Frage, z. B. „Wann fährt der nächste Zug?“

Während des Hörens:
Mach dir Notizen.
1. Falls du dir mehrere Punkte notieren willst, kannst du eine Liste, eine *mind map* oder eine Tabelle anfertigen.
2. Hör dir den Text bei einer Prüfung zwei- oder dreimal an. Im Alltag ist das nicht möglich, aber dann kannst du immer jemanden fragen.
3. Prüfe, ob du alle Infos hast, die du brauchst.

Nach dem Hören:
Erledige sämtliche Aufgaben mithilfe deiner Notizen. Falls du mit einem Partner / einer Partnerin zusammenarbeitest, vergleicht eure Ergebnisse.

11 Ein Interview mit jemandem führen

Bevor du ein Interview führst, ist es wichtig, dass du versuchst im Voraus etwas über die Person bzw. das Thema zu erfahren. So kannst du leichter Fragen stellen. Das Interview wird dadurch interessanter.

Tipps	**Im Studio**	**Auf der Straße**
1. Be polite.		
	 Good morning / afternoon … My name is / I'm … Thank you for coming to the studio / …	Excuse me. I'm from … School. May I ask you a question about / your opinion on …? 
2. Prepare your questions.		
Beginne mit einem Fragewort.	***Who** do you …?/ **What** have you …?/ **Why** did you …?*	***What** is your opinion on …?*
Beginne mit einem Verb.	***Can** you tell me …?/ **Have** you ever …?/**Is** it true that …?*	***Do** you think people should …? **Can** you remember …?*
Beginne mit einer höflichen Einladung / Aufforderung.	***Please, tell** us about … / **explain** …*	***Could you** say something about …? **Would you** be prepared to give us your opinion on …?*
3. Say goodbye.		
Bedanke dich und sage noch etwas Nettes.	***Thank you** very much … That was very interesting / … **We hope** you enjoy your stay in …*	***Thank you** Sir / Madam / … You have been very helpful. **Have a nice day.***

12 Eine Präsentation vorbereiten

1. Schreibt zunächst ein Handout und macht Kopien für die Klasse.
   Hier ein Beispiel:

The title →	*Deadly creatures*	← Schreibt den Titel als Überschrift auf die Seite.
Part A Important words →	*Important words* *shark = Hai* *snake =*	← Wählt 10–12 wichtige Wörter bzw. Wendungen aus und erstellt eine Wortliste.
Part B Facts →	*Facts* *The Great White Shark is …*	← Schreibt 5–6 wichtige Fakten auf.
Part C Notes →	*Lots of dangerous … in …*	← Lasst Platz für Notizen.

2. Wählt eine Präsentationsform, die ihr interessant findet und bei der ihr eure Talente am besten anwenden könnt. Hier ein paar Beispiele:

A display (talents: drawing, designing)

A demonstration (talents: making / explaining things)

A sales talk (talents: public speaking)

A discussion (talents: speaking, working in a group)

A performance (talents: singing, performing, acting)

A computer presentation (talents: using equipment, typing)

Weitere Präsentationsformen, die ihr in diesem Buch findet, sind: *a web page, an advert, an interview, a talk show, a PowerPoint presentation, a reading, a quiz, a summary, a report, a talk, a gallery walk.*

3. Tipps für eine PowerPoint-Präsentation:

Tipps

1. Plan your presentation on paper first.
2. Write down a title.
3. Write down the aspects of the topic as a list.
4. Write a few key words on each aspect.
5. Start your PowerPoint programme.
6. Type the title on to one 'page' and your key words on to the other 'pages'. Use your key words in sentences during your presentation.
7. Use pictures and diagrams to improve your presentation.

4. Überprüft, ob eure Mitschüler / innen alles verstanden haben, was ihr ihnen gezeigt bzw. erzählt habt.

A written test	Das können z. B. Fragen, ein Lückentext, ein beschriftetes Diagramm, ein Quiz, ein Kreuzworträtsel, ein Fehlertext bzw. ein Fehlerbild sein.
An oral test	Spiele aller Art: Rollenspiele, Ratespiele, Nacherzählungen, Interviews, Zusammenfassungen, … , z. B.: Ein Kartenspiel: Schreibe Fragen auf Kärtchen. Die anderen ziehen eine Karte und beantworten die Frage.

13 Eine Diskussion / Debatte durchführen

Es gibt viele verschiedene Arten einer Diskussion / Debatte. Folgende Tipps und Redewendungen können euch helfen:

	Tipps	Ausdrücke
1	Einigt euch auf eine Aussage (*statement / motion*).	*I think … is a good statement.* *I'd like to suggest … as our statement.* *Let's vote on it. Who's for / against the statement …*
2	Schreibt sie an die Tafel.	*Statement: Everybody should work for a short time in another country.*
3	Wer macht den Vorsitz? Er / Sie muss die Diskussion / Debatte mithilfe der Sätze rechts leiten.	*Good morning / afternoon.* *Our statement for today's discussion is: …* *Speakers for / against the statement are …* *The first speaker for / against the statement is …* *… , it's your turn. You may speak now.* *Thank you … . Your time is up.*
4	Die Sprecher sammeln Argumente für und gegen die Aussage.	*I agree / don't agree with the statement.* *In my opinion …* *I think it is wrong / important to say that …*
5	Der / Die Vorsitzende fragt, ob andere ihre Meinung äußern möchten.	*Yes, … , what would you like to say?*
6	Der / Die Vorsitzende beendet die Diskussion / Debatte und fordert zur Abstimmung auf.	*Please raise your hand if you are for / against the statement.* *The results of the vote are … for and … against the statement.*

14 Think-Pair-Share (T-P-S)

Du liest und hörst in der Klasse oft: *Compare your answers with a partner, then report to the class.* Dies wird *Think-Pair-Share* genannt.
So funktioniert es:

- Mach dir Gedanken zu der Aufgabe und notiere sie. Dein Lehrer kann dir eine zeitliche Grenze von z. B. 5 Minuten geben.
- Finde eine/n Partner/in. Lest euch eure Notizen gegenseitig vor. Zeig sie deinem/r Partner/in nicht! Dies ist eine Sprechaktivität.
- Korrigiert eure Notizen, wenn ihr einen Fehler findet oder fügt neue Informationen hinzu, wenn eine/r von euch eine bessere Idee hat.
- Du oder dein/e Partner/in präsentiert eure gemeinsamen Ideen der Klasse, oder wenn die Aufgabe lang genug ist, stellt ihr sie beide abwechselnd vor.

15 Cheat sheet

Cheat sheet heißt auf Deutsch *Spickzettel* und ist eine gute Möglichkeit, einen Text zusammenzufassen und eine kurze Präsentation darüber zu halten. So funktioniert es:

- Geh den Text durch und notiere Schlüsselbegriffe und wichtige Ausdrücke auf ein kleines Stück Papier. Diese Schlüsselbegriffe enthalten die wichtigsten Informationen des Textes.
- Gehe deine Notizen durch und streiche alle Wörter durch, die nicht absolut notwendig sind! Idealerweise solltest du nur einen Schlüsselbegriff für jeden Teil des Textes haben.
- Verwende deine Liste *(cheat sheet)*, um deine Präsentation zu halten. Die Schlüsselbegriffe helfen dir, dir zu merken, was du sagen willst, aber du solltest soweit wie möglich deine eigenen Worte benutzen. Wiederhole nicht einfach den Originaltext!

16 Gallery walk

Am Ende vieler Gruppenarbeiten in der Klasse werdet ihr einen Text, z. B. eine E-Mail oder vielleicht ein Poster produziert haben. Ein *gallery walk* ist eine Möglichkeit, eure Arbeitsergebnisse in der Klasse zu zeigen. So funktioniert es:

- Hängt die Ergebnisse aller Gruppen im Klassenraum auf und verteilt sie soweit voneinander entfernt wie möglich.
- Dann schaut ihr euch jede Gruppenarbeit im Klassenzimmer an.
- Wenn du bei deiner Arbeit angekommen bist, halte dort an und sei bereit, sie zu erklären und Fragen der Klasse hierzu zu beantworten. Jede/r in deiner Gruppe sollte hierzu in der Lage sein.
- Fahrt in dieser Weise fort, bis jede/r alle Arbeiten gesehen hat.
- Zum Schluss diskutiert ihr die Ergebnisse in der Klasse. Welches war das beliebteste / interessanteste / am besten präsentierte? Warum?

Grundwortschatz und Zahlen

Wochentage, Monatsnamen, Subjektpronomen (*he, she, it* usw.) und Wörter, die im Deutschen und Englischen ähnlich oder identisch sind (z. B. *jeans*), werden als bekannt vorausgesetzt und sind im Folgenden nicht aufgeführt.

A

a/an ein(e)
about über; ungefähr
activity Aktivität
address Adresse
after nach
afternoon Nachmittag
again wieder
against gegen
age Alter
airport Flughafen
all alle(s)
already schon, bereits
also auch
always immer
a.m. vormittags *(nur nach Uhrzeiten)*
America Amerika
American amerikanisch; Amerikaner/in
and und
animal Tier
another noch eine(r, s), ein(e) andere(r, s)
answer; to answer Antwort; beantworten
any irgendein(e)
apple Apfel
to arrive ankommen
as als
to ask (questions) fragen, (Fragen) stellen
at an, auf, in, bei
at home zu Hause
autumn Herbst
away weg

B

back zurück
bad schlecht, schlimm
bathroom Badezimmer
to be (was/were, been) sein
beach Strand
beautiful schön
because weil
bed Bett
bedroom Schlafzimmer
to begin (began, begun) anfangen
below unter, unten
best beste(r, s)
better besser
big groß
bike/bicycle Fahrrad
bird Vogel
birthday Geburtstag
bit (a bit) (ein) bisschen
black schwarz
blue blau
book Buch
boring langweilig
bottle Flasche
box Schachtel, Kiste, Kasten, Kästchen
boy Junge
boyfriend Freund
bread Brot
breakfast Frühstück
Britain Großbritannien
British britisch
brother Bruder
bus Bus
but aber
to bring (brought, brought) bringen
to buy (bought, bought) kaufen
by von; mit

C

cake Kuchen
called namens
can können
car Auto
cat Katze
centre Zentrum
chair Stuhl
child, children Kind(er)
cinema Kino
city (Groß)stadt
class (Schul)klasse, Kurs
clock (Wand)uhr
coffee Kaffee
coke Cola
cold kalt
colour Farbe
to come (came, come) kommen
to cook kochen
to copy kopieren, abschreiben
correct; to correct korrekt, richtig; korrigieren
to cost (cost, cost) kosten
to count zählen
country, countries Land, Länder
to cover decken, bedecken, abdecken
cupboard Schrank

D

dad Papa
to dance tanzen
dancer Tänzer/in
date Datum
daughter Tochter
day Tag
desk Schreibtisch
dialogue Dialog
dictionary Wörterbuch
different verschieden, unterschiedlich
difficult schwierig, schwer
dinner Abendessen
to do (did, done) machen, tun
dog Hund
door Tür
drink; to drink (drank, drunk) Getränk, Trinken; trinken

E

ear Ohr
early früh
east Ost
easy leicht
to eat (ate, eaten) essen
egg Ei
English Englisch; englisch
evening Abend
every jede(r,s)
everywhere überall
example; for example Beispiel; zum Beispiel
Excuse me! Entschuldigung!
exercise Übung
expensive teuer
eye Auge

F

false falsch
family Familie
famous berühmt
far weit, fern
fast schnell
father Vater
favourite lieblings-
to feel (felt, felt) fühlen
to fill in ausfüllen
to find (found, found) finden
to find out herausfinden
fine fein, schön
finish beenden, abschließen, fertigstellen
firm Firma
first erste(r, s)
fish Fisch
flower Blume, Blüte
to fly (flew, flown) fliegen
food Essen, Nahrung
foot, feet Fuß, Füße
football Fußball
for für
to forget (forgot, forgotten) vergessen
form Form; Formular
free frei, kostenlos
free time Freizeit
friend Freund
friendly freundlich
from von
fruit Obst
full voll, vollständig
fun Spaß

G

game Spiel
garden Garten
German Deutsch; deutsch
Germany Deutschland
to get (got, got) bekommen, erhalten
to get up aufstehen
girl Mädchen
girlfriend Freundin
to give (gave, given) geben
glass Glas
to go (went, gone) gehen
good gut
good morning guten Morgen
goodbye auf Wiedersehen
grass Gras, Rasen
great großartig
green grün
guitar Gitarre

guy Typ, Kerl
guest Gast

H

hair Haar
half halb
hand Hand
to happen geschehen, passieren
happy glücklich
hard hart, schwierig
hat Hut
to hate hassen, gar nicht mögen
to have (had, had) haben
head Kopf
to hear (heard, heard) hören
hello hallo
help; to help Hilfe; helfen
her ihr(e)
here hier
hi hallo
high hoch
him ihm, ihn
his sein(e)
holiday Urlaub, Ferien
home Zuhause
homework Hausaufgabe
hot heiß, scharf
hour Stunde
house Haus
how many wie viele
how old wie alt
hungry hungrig
husband Ehemann

I

idea Idee, Vorstellung
if wenn, falls, ob
important wichtig
in; into in; in ... hinein
in front of vor
interested (in) interessiert (an)
interesting interessant
its sein(e), ihr(e)

J

job Arbeit, Beruf
just einfach, nur, gerade

K

kid Kind
kilometre Kilometer
to know (knew, known) wissen, kennen

L

language Sprache
large weit, groß
last letzte(r, s)
late (zu) spät
to learn lernen, erfahren
left links
lesson Unterrichtsstunde
Let's ... Lass/lasst uns ...
letter Brief
light Licht; leicht
like wie
to like mögen
life, lives Leben
to listen (zu)hören
little klein, wenig
to live leben, wohnen
living room Wohnzimmer
long lang
to look at betrachten, ansehen
lots of, a lot of viel(e)
loud laut
to love lieben, sehr gern mögen
lunch Mittagessen

M

magazine Zeitschrift
to make (made, made) machen
man, men Mann, Männer
many viele
map (Land)karte
me mir, mich
to mean (meant, meant) bedeuten
meal Mahlzeit
to meet (met, met) treffen, kennen lernen
metre Meter
midday Mittag
middle Mitte; mittlere(r, s)
midnight Mitternacht
mile Meile
milk Milch
minute Minute
mistake Fehler
(at the) moment (im) Moment
money Geld
month Monat
more mehr
morning Morgen
most die meisten
mother Mutter
motor bike Motorrad
movie *(US)* Kinofilm
Mr Herr (Anrede)
Mrs Frau (Anrede für verheiratete Frau)
Ms Frau (Anrede)
mum Mama
music Musik
must müssen
my mein(e)

N

name Name
near nahe
never nie(mals)
new neu
next nächste(r, s)
nice nett, schön, hübsch
night Nacht
no nein; kein/e
noise Lärm, Geräusch
north Nord
not nicht
nothing nichts
now jetzt
number Zahl, Nummer

O

o'clock Uhr
of von, aus
of course natürlich
office Büro
often oft, häufig
old alt
on an, auf, bei, in
one day eines Tages
only nur, erst
open; to open offen, geöffnet; öffnen
or oder
other andere(r,s)
our unser(e)

P

p.m. nachmittags (nur nach Uhrzeiten)
page Seite
paper Papier
parents Eltern
part Teil
partner Partner(in)
to pay (paid, paid) (be)zahlen
pen Stift, Füller
people Leute, Volk
perhaps vielleicht
person Person
phone Telefon
photo(graph) Foto(graf)
picture Bild
place Platz, Ort, Stelle
plane Flugzeug
to play spielen
please bitte
police Polizei
potato Kartoffel
pound Pfund
price Preis
to put (put, put) setzen, legen, stellen

Q

quarter Viertel
question Frage
quick(ly) schnell
quiz Ratespiel

R

rain; to rain Regen; regnen
to read (read, read); read out lesen; vorlesen
really wirklich
red rot
remember sich erinnern, daran denken
rich reich
to ride (rode, ridden) reiten; fahren *(mit dem Auto, Fahrrad)*
right richtig; rechts
right now gerade jetzt
river Fluss
road Straße
room Zimmer, Raum
to run (ran, run) laufen, rennen

S

sad traurig
same der-/die-/dasselbe
to say (said, said) sagen
school Schule
Scotland Schottland
secretary Sekretärin
sea Meer
second zweite(r, s)
to see (saw, seen) sehen, verstehen
to sell verkaufen
to send (sent, sent) schicken, senden
sentence Satz
sheep Schaf
shoe Schuh
shop Geschäft, Laden
shopping Einkaufen
short kurz
to shut (shut, shut) schließen
to sing (sang, sung) singen
sister Schwester
to sit (sat, sat) sitzen
to sleep (slept, slept) schlafen
slow langsam
small klein
snow Schnee
so so
some einige

something etwas
sometimes manchmal
son Sohn
song Lied
soon bald
(I'm) sorry. Tut mir Leid.
south Süden
to speak (spoke, spoken) sprechen
spring Frühling
to stand (stood, stood) stehen
to start anfangen, beginnen
story Geschichte
street Straße
strong stark, kräftig
student Schüler(in), Student(in)
suddenly plötzlich
sugar Zucker
summer Sommer
sun Sonne
sure sicher
to swim (swam, swum) schwimmen

T

table Tabelle, Tisch
to take (took, taken) nehmen, brauchen, dauern
to talk reden, sprechen
tall groß
tea Tea
teacher Lehrer(in)
television Fernsehen
to tell (told, told) erzählen, sagen
thanks; thank you danke
that der/die/das
their ihr(e)
them sie, ihnen
then dann
there dort
there is/are es gibt
these diese
thing Ding, Sache
to think (thought, thought) denken, glauben, meinen
third dritte
this diese(r, s)
those diese
time Zeit
times Mal
tired müde
to an, auf, nach, zu
today heute
tomorrow morgen
too auch; zu
town Stadt
train Zug
to travel reisen, fahren
tree Baum
trousers Hose
true wahr, echt
to try versuchen

U

under unter
to understand (understood, understood) verstehen
to use benutzen, verwenden
usually gewöhnlich

V

very sehr
to visit besuchen

W

to wait warten
to wake up (woke, woken) aufwachen, aufwecken
to walk gehen, laufen, spazieren
wall Wand
to want wollen
to wash waschen
to watch beobachten, zuschauen
water Wasser
to wear (wore, worn) tragen
weather Wetter
week Woche
weekend Wochenende
welcome willkommen
well gut; gesund; also
west Westen
what was
what time um wie viel Uhr
when wann
where wo
which welche(r, s)
white weiß
who wer, wem, wen
why warum
wife, wives Ehefrau, Ehefrauen
to win (won, won) gewinnen
window Fenster
winter Winter
with mit, bei
without ohne
woman, women Frau, Frauen
wonderful herrlich, traumhaft, wundervoll
word Wort
work; to work Arbeit; arbeiten
world Welt
to write (wrote, written) schreiben
wrong falsch

Y

year Jahr
years old Jahre alt
yellow gelb
yes ja
yesterday gestern
young jung
your dein(e), euer/eure

Zahlen

Cardinal numbers				Ordinal numbers			
1	one	17	seventeen	1st	first	17th	seventeenth
2	two	18	eighteen	2nd	second	18th	eighteenth
3	three	19	nineteen	3rd	third	19th	nineteenth
4	four	20	twenty	4th	fourth	20th	twentieth
5	five	21	twenty-one	5th	fifth	21st	twenty-first
6	six	22	twenty-two	6th	sixth	22nd	twenty-second
7	seven	30	thirty	7th	seventh	30th	thirtieth
8	eight	31	thirty-one	8th	eighth	31st	thirty-first
9	nine	40	forty	9th	ninth	40th	fortieth
10	ten	50	fifty	10th	tenth	50th	fiftieth
11	eleven	60	sixty	11th	eleventh	60th	sixtieth
12	twelve	70	seventy	12th	twelfth	70th	seventieth
13	thirteen	80	eighty	13th	thirteenth	80th	eightieth
14	fourteen	90	ninety	14th	fourteenth	90th	ninetieth
15	fifteen	100	a hundred	15th	fifteenth	100th	hundredth
16	sixteen	110	a hundred and ten	16th	sixteenth		

1,000 a thousand · **1,000,000 (1m)** a million · **1,000,000,000 (1bn)** a billion
1.5 one point five • **2.73** two point seven three · **27%** twenty-seven per cent
½ a half · ¼ a quarter · ¾ three quarters · ⅓ a third · ⅕ a fifth
£1.50 one pound fifty · **99p** ninety-nine p/pence · $12.20 twelve dollars twenty

Unitbegleitendes Vokabular

Videotraining: Englische Aussprache

Perfekte englische Aussprache leicht gemacht: Mit dem Lernprogramm zur englischen Lautschrift können Sie alle Laute einüben. Wählen Sie einfach in der Navigation rechts den entsprechenden Reiter (*Vowels* oder *Consonants*) aus und klicken Sie dann auf das gewünschte phonetische Symbol. Sprechen Sie die Wörter laut nach.

Unter www.klett.de geben Sie bitte den Code unter der Abbildung rechts ein.

n633sn

Abkürzungen und Zeichen

etw = etwa
pl = Plural, Mehrzahl
sb = somebody
sth = something
BE = britisches Englisch
AE = amerikanisches Englisch
AustrE = australisches Englisch
NewZE = neuseeländisches Englisch

L = links
R = rechts

= entspricht
↔ ist das Gegenteil von
→ verwandt mit
! Achtung

1A Vor den Vokabeln findest du immer die jeweiligen Übungsnummern der Unit.

blue Vokabel aus Hörtext

Entry English, English everywhere

	entry ['entri]	Zugang	
1A	**Cologne** [kə'ləʊn]	Köln	
	Europe ['jʊərəp]	Europa	
	USA [ˌju:es'eɪ]	Vereinigte Staaten von Amerika	the United States of America
1B	**What about you?** [ˌwɒt əbaʊt 'ju:]	Und du?	
	London ['lʌndən]	Hauptstadt Englands	
	England ['ɪŋglənd]	England	
1C	**to take it in turns** [ˌteɪk ɪt ɪn 'tɜ:nz]	sich abwechseln	There's only one bathroom. We must take it in turns.
2A	**native speaker** [ˌneɪtɪv 'spi:kə]	Muttersprachler/in	
	Canada ['kænədə]	Kanada	
	G'day [g'deɪ]	(AustrE:) Guten Tag!	
	nurse [nɜ:s]	Krankenschwester, Krankenpfleger	Nurses work in hospitals.
	construction worker [kən'strʌkʃn wɜ:kə]	Bauarbeiter/in	
2B	**technician** [tek'nɪʃn]	Techniker/in	*-ician* für Berufe *(electrician, musician)*
2C	**New Zealand** [ˌnju: 'zi:lənd]	Neuseeland	
	twins [twɪnz]	Zwillinge	
	painter ['peɪntə]	Maler/in, Anstreicher/in	painter → to paint
	decorator ['dekəreɪtə]	Maler/in, Tapezierer/in	
	doctor ['dɒktə]	Arzt, Ärztin	You go to the doctor when you are ill.

	doctor's receptionist ['dɒktəz rɪ'sepʃənɪst]	Sprechstundenhilfe	
2E	**Australia** [ɒs'treɪlɪə]	Australien	
	to be called [bi 'kɔ:ld]	heißen	
3A	**Montana** [mɒn'tænə]	US-Bundesstaat	
	walking ['wɔ:kɪŋ]	Wandern, Spazierengehen	walking ↔ running
	cycling ['saɪklɪŋ]	Fahrradfahren	I love walking and cycling.
	canoeing [kə'nu:ɪŋ]	Kanufahren	
	to go on holiday [ˌgəʊ ɒn 'hɒlɪdeɪ]	Urlaub machen (in)	They go on holiday to Italy every year.
3B	**hostel** ['hɒstl]	Herberge	
	brochure ['brəʊʃə]	Prospekt, Broschüre	! Betonung
	on the phone [ˌɒn ðə 'fəʊn]	am Telefon	
	hostel warden ['hɒstl wɔ:dn]	Herbergsvater/-mutter	
	to complete [kəm'pli:t]	vervollständigen	Complete the sentences with a partner.
	to check [tʃek]	überprüfen, kontrollieren	Can you check the time? Isn't it late?
	mountain ['maʊntɪn]	Berg	
	speaking ['spi:kɪŋ]	am Apparat	
	facilities [fə'sɪlətɪz]	Einrichtung(en), Räumlichkeiten, Ausstattung	The hotel has fantastic facilities.
	dining room ['daɪnɪŋ rʊm]	Esszimmer, Speisesaal	
	washing machine ['wɒʃɪŋ məʃi:n]	Waschmaschine	There's a washing machine for dirty T-shirts.
	thanks very much [ˌθæŋks veri 'mʌtʃ]	vielen Dank	Thanks very much for your help.
	You're welcome [jɔ: 'welkəm]	Bitte. Gern geschehen.	
	bye [baɪ]	tschüs	→ bye-bye
	access ['ækses]	Zugang, Zugriff	I have access to his computer.
	etc. [et 'setərə]	usw.	
	to contact ['kɒntækt]	sich in Verbindung setzen mit	If you want to contact her, write an email.
3C	**swimming pool** ['swɪmɪŋ pu:l]	Schwimmbad	
	movie theater ['mu:vi θɪətə]	(AE:) Kino	
	main [meɪn]	Haupt-	
	post office ['pəʊst ɒfɪs]	Postamt	Get me some stamps at the post office.
	pharmacy ['fɑ:məsi]	(AE:) Apotheke	(BE:) chemist
4A	**celeb** [sɪ'leb]	Promi	
	star [stɑ:]	Star	the star of the show
	sportspeople ['spɔ:tspi:pl]	Sportler	
	singer ['sɪŋə]	Sänger/in	singer → to sing
	musician [mjʊ'zɪʃn]	Musiker/in	musician → music → musical
	celebrity [sɪ'lebrɪti]	Prominente/r	There were many celebrities at the party.
	Munich ['mju:nɪk]	München	
	footballer ['fʊtbɔ:lə]	Fußballspieler/in	
	to note down [ˌnəʊt 'daʊn]	notieren, aufschreiben	Listen and note down your answers.
	France [frɑ:ns]	Frankreich	
	piano [pɪ'ænəʊ]	Klavier	
	tattoo [tæt'u:]	Tätowierung	
	side [saɪd]	Seite	They drive on the left side of the road in Britain.
	body ['bɒdi]	Körper	
	back ['bæk]	Rücken	She has a tattoo on her back.
	actor ['æktə]	Schauspieler	actor → actress
	California [kælɪ'fɔ:niə]	Kalifornien	
	once [wʌns]	einmal	I only did it once.
4C	**questionnaire** [ˌkwestʃə'neə]	Fragebogen	The questionnaire has 100 questions.
	motor bike ['məʊtə baɪk]	Motorrad	
	scooter ['sku:tə]	Motorroller	He rides a scooter to work.
	inline skates ['ɪnlaɪn skeɪts]	Inline-Skates	
	laptop ['læptɒp]	Laptop, Notebook	
	album ['ælbəm]	Album, CD, Schallplatte	
	poster ['pəʊstə]	Plakat	

	musical instrument [ˌmju:zɪkl ˈɪnstrəmənt]	Musikinstrument	
4D	**No way!** [ˌnəʊ ˈweɪ]	Nie im Leben! Auf gar keinen Fall!	No way! I won't go to her concert.
	terrible [ˈterəbl]	furchtbar, fürchterlich	The music was terrible!
	verb [vɜ:b]	Verb	
5A	**to match** [mætʃ]	zuordnen	Match the numbers and letters.
	to [tə]	(Uhrzeit:) vor	
	a quarter to [ə ˈkwɔ:tə tə]	(Uhrzeit:) Viertel vor	quarter wird wie four ausgesprochen
5B	**to point to** [pɔɪnt ˈtə]	zeigen auf	Point to the right number.
	What time is it? [ˌwɒt ˈtaɪm ɪz ɪt]	Wie spät ist es? Wieviel Uhr ist es?	
5C	**social** [ˈsəʊʃl]	sozial	
	networking [ˈnetwɜ:kɪŋ]	Netzwerk(-)	
	site [saɪt]	Website	
	missing [ˈmɪsɪŋ]	fehlend	There's a letter missing.
	fashion [ˈfæʃn]	Mode	
	company [ˈkʌmpəni]	Unternehmen, Firma	firm
	to jog [dʒɒg]	joggen	
	to start [stɑ:t]	starten	to start ↔ to stop
	to say 'hello' to sb [ˌseɪ həˌləʊ tə]	jdn begrüßen	Say 'hello' to my mother.
	apartment [əˈpɑ:tmənt]	(AE:) Wohnung	(BE:) flat
5D	**tip** [tɪp]	Tipp, Hinweis	
	trick [trɪk]	Trick, Kniff	
	subway [ˈsʌbweɪ]	(AE:) U-Bahn	(BE:) underground
	supper [ˈsʌpə]	Abendessen	Supper is at 6 o'clock.
5E	**to work out** [wɜ:k ˈaʊt]	trainieren	
	fitness club [ˈfɪtnəs klʌb]	Fitnessklub	
5F	**vocational college** [vəʊˌkeɪʃnl ˈkɒlɪdʒ]	Berufsbildende Schule	
6A	**waiter** [ˈweɪtə]	Kellner	waiter → waitress
	bus driver [ˈbʌs draɪvə]	Busfahrer/in	
	shoe shop [ˈʃu: ʃɒp]	Schuhgeschäft	
	receptionist [rɪˈsepʃənɪst]	Empfangsdame, -mitarbeiter	receptionist → reception
	shop assistant [ˈʃɒp əsɪstənt]	Verkäufer/in	A shop assistant sells things in the shop.
	mechanic [mɪˈkænɪk]	Mechaniker/in	A mechanic often works with cars.
	backpacker [ˈbækpækə]	Rucksacktourist/in	
6B	**conversation** [ˌkɒnvəˈseɪʃn]	Gespräch, Unterhaltung	a conversation with sb about sth
	trainers [ˈtreɪnəz]	Turnschuhe	
	Just a minute! [ˌdʒʌst ə ˈmɪnɪt]	Einen Moment!	
	should [ʃʊd]	sollte/n	It's cold. You should wear a pullover.
	thanks a lot [ˌθæŋks ə ˈlɒt]	vielen Dank	
	ticket [ˈtɪkɪt]	Fahrschein	Buy a ticket, then take the bus.
	euro [ˈjʊərəʊ]	Euro	! Betonung
	to sit down [sɪt ˈdaʊn]	sich (hin)setzen	to sit down ↔ to stand up
	to go off [gəʊ ˈɒf]	losgehen	
	most of the time [ˈməʊst əv ðə ˌtaɪm]	meistens	usually
	maybe [ˈmeɪbi]	vielleicht	perhaps
	to stop [stɒp]	anhalten, stehen bleiben, (Motor:) ausgehen	The bus always stops here.
	engine [ˈendʒɪn]	Motor	Most cars have the engine in the front.
	electrical [ɪˈlektrɪkl]	elektrisch	
	ready [ˈredi]	bereit, fertig	If you are ready, let's go.
	to order [ˈɔ:də]	bestellen	Let's order steaks.
	yeah [jeə]	ja	
	menu [ˈmenju:]	Speisekarte	! Nicht verwechseln mit 'Menü'.
	steak [steɪk]	Steak	
	fries [fraɪz]	(AE:) Pommes	(BE:) chips
	vegetables [ˈvedʒtəblz]	Gemüse	! Betonung

	pea [piː]	Erbse	
	carrot ['kærət]	Karotte, Möhre	
	bean [biːn]	Bohne	
	medium rare [ˌmiːdiəm 'reə]	(Steak:) medium	medium – rare – well done
	certainly ['sɜːtnli]	gewiss, sicherlich	I certainly want to come to your birthday party.
	credit card ['kredɪt ˌkɑːd]	Kreditkarte	
	to reserve [rɪ'sɜːv]	reservieren	Can I reserve a table?
	to call [kɔːl]	anrufen	to phone
	to look forward to doing [ˌlʊk 'fɔːwəd tə]	sich auf etw freuen	I look forward to hearing from you.
6C	**youth** [juːθ]	Jugend	young people
	youth hostel ['juːθ hɒstl]	Jugendherberge	A youth hostel is a cheap place to stay.
	size [saɪz]	Größe	What size shoes do you take?
	to book [bʊk]	reservieren, buchen	I want to book a holiday in Italy.
7A	**capital city** [ˌkæpɪtl 'sɪti]	Hauptstadt	London is the capital of the United Kingdom.
	cook [kʊk]	Koch/Köchin	
	crown [kraʊn]	Krone	
	at work [ət 'wɜːk]	bei der Arbeit	He's not here. He's at work.
	to welcome ['welkəm]	wilkommen heißen, begrüßen	
	much [mʌtʃ]	viel	
	from around the world [frəm əˌraund ðə 'wɜːld]	aus der ganzen Welt	
	married to ['mærɪd to]	verheiratet mit	He's married to my sister.
	twice [twaɪs]	zweimal	Listen. I won't tell you twice.
	to surf [sɜːf]	surfen	
7C	**to imagine** [ɪ'mædʒɪn]	sich etw vorstellen	It's difficult to imagine, but it's true.
7D	**phrase** [freɪz]	Wendung, Ausdruck	
	single room ['sɪŋgl ˌruːm]	Einzelzimmer	
	double room ['dʌbl ˌruːm]	Doppelzimmer	
	sir [sɜː]	mein Herr	Good morning, sir.
7F	**next to** ['nekst tə]	neben	Can I sit next to you?
7G	**to test** [test]	testen, ausprobieren	
	to choose [tʃuːz, tʃəʊz, tʃəʊzən]	wählen, auswählen, aussuchen	! Doppel 'o'
	past [pɑːst]	(Uhrzeit:) nach	! half past twelve = halb eins
	to watch TV [ˌwɒtʃ tiː'viː]	fernsehen	to watch TV – to see a film
	horse [hɔːs]	Pferd	

Unit 1 At college

unit ['juːnɪt]	Lektion	
college ['kɒlɪdʒ]	Hochschule, Berufsbildende Schule, Universität	After school you can go to college.
to search ['sɜːtʃ]	suchen, durchsuchen	
worldwide [wɜːld'waɪd]	auf der ganzen Welt, weltweit	The company has offices worldwide.
platform ['plætfɔːm]	Plattform	
community [kə'mjuːnəti]	Gemeinde	It's a very friendly community here.
community college [kə'mjuːnəti kɒlɪdʒ]	(AE:) College zur Berufsausbildung und Vorbereitung auf ein Hochschulstudium	
to get to know [ˌget tə 'nəʊ)]	kennen lernen	After a week we got to know everybody well.
around the world [əˌraund ðə 'wɜːld]	auf der ganzen Welt	
to organise ['ɔːgənaɪz]	organisieren	We must organise a meeting as soon as possible.
project ['prɒdʒekt]	Projekt	
between [bɪ'twiːn]	zwischen	There's a break between lessons.
international [ˌɪntə'næʃnl]	international	
visit ['vɪzɪt]	Besuch	visit → to visit → visitor
exchange [ɪks'tʃeɪndʒ]	Austausch	

1B	**message** ['mesɪdʒ]	Nachricht, Mitteilung	
	particularly [pə'tɪkjələli]	vor allem, insbesondere	This is particularly important.
2A	**full-time** ['fʊl taɪm]	Ganztags-, Vollzeit-	full-time ↔ part-time
	business course ['bɪznəs kɔ:s]	Betriebswirtschaftslehrgang	
	course [kɔ:s]	Kurs, Lehrgang	
	marketing company ['mɑ:kətɪŋ kʌmpəni]	Vertriebsgesellschaft	
	break [breɪk]	Pause	Let's have a break for lunch.
	athletics [æθ'letɪks]	Leichtathletik	athletics → athlete
2C	**simple present** [ˌsɪmpl 'preznt]	einfaches Präsens	
2D	**truck** [trʌk]	(AE:) Lkw, Lastwagen	(BE:) lorry
	truck driver ['trʌk draɪvə]	(AE:) Lastwagenfahrer/in, Fernfahrer/in	
	state [steɪt]	Staat, Bundesstaat	
	to flow [fləʊ]	fließen	
3A	**almost** ['ɔ:lməʊst]	fast, beinah	Emma is still 17, but she's almost 18.
	to leave (left, left) [li:v, left, left]	weggehen, verlassen, (von der Schule) abgehen	
	one day [wʌn 'deɪ]	eines Tages	
3B	**to offer** ['ɒfə]	bieten, anbieten	Can I offer you a drink?
	to train [treɪn]	eine Ausbildung machen	
	to last [lɑ:st]	dauern	The hot weather doesn't usually last that long.
3A	**over** ['əʊvə]	über	
	everyone ['evriwʌn]	jeder, alle	everybody
	whether ['weðə]	ob	Nicht verwechseln mit *weather*.
	hairdresser ['heəˌdresə]	Friseur/in	Hairdressers wash and cut people's hair.
	enough [ɪ'nʌf]	genug, genügend	Die zweite Silbe wird 'aff' gesprochen.
	credit ['kredɪt]	etwa: Leistungspunkte	
	even ['i:vn]	sogar, noch	She is tall, but her brother is even taller.
	to need [ni:d]	brauchen, benötigen	Tom needs a lot of sleep.
	details ['di:teɪlz]	Einzelheiten, Angaben	
	subject ['sʌbdʒɪkt]	Fach, Thema	
	area ['eəriə]	Gebiet	
	art [ɑ:t]	Kunst, Graphic	**!** Nicht mit 'Art' verwechseln.
	design [dɪ'zaɪn]	Gestaltung, Design	
	automotive mechanics [ɔ:təˌməʊtɪv mi:'kænɪks]	Kraftfahrzeugmechanik	
	business administration ['bɪznəs ədmɪnɪstreɪʃn]	Betriebswirtschaftslehre	
	administration [ədˌmɪnɪ'streɪʃn]	Verwaltung	administration → to administer
	information technology [ɪnfəˌmeɪʃn tek'nɒlədʒi]	Informationstechnologie	IT is short for information technology.
	construction [kən'strʌkʃn]	Baugewerbe, Bauwesen	construction → to construct
	health [helθ]	Gesundheit, Gesundheitswesen	health → healthy
	beauty ['bju:ti]	Schönheit, Kosmetik	beauty → beautiful
	media ['mi:dɪə]	Medien	
	to email ['i:meɪl]	eine E-Mail schreiben	
	retail services ['ri:teɪl sɜ:vɪsɪz]	Einzelhandel	
	social work [ˌsəʊʃl 'wɜ:k]	Sozialarbeit	
	child care ['tʃaɪld keə]	Kinderbetreuung	
	toll free ['təʊl fri:]	(AE:) gebührenfrei	
	electronics [ɪˌlek'trɒnɪks]	Elektronik	There are many electronics companies in Asia.
4A	**lunch break** ['lʌntʃ breɪk]	Mittagspause	
4B	**normally** ['nɔ:mli]	üblicherweise, normalerweise	
	to hang out with (hung, hung) [ˌhæŋ 'aʊt wɪð, hʌŋ, hʌŋ]	mit jdm abhängen, sich mit jdm rumtreiben	
4C	**uncle** ['ʌŋkl]	Onkel	aunt and uncle
	radio station ['reɪdɪəʊ steɪʃn]	Radiosender	

	technical ['teknɪkl]	technisch	technical → technician
	mall [mɔ:l]	Einkaufszentrum	Teenagers love hanging out at malls.
4D	**information** [ˌɪnfə'meɪʃn]	Angaben, Information(en)	a piece of information, some information
	astronaut ['æstrənɔ:t]	Astronaut/in	
	negative ['negətɪv]	verneinend, negativ	
4E	**extremely** [ɪk'stri:mli]	äußerst	The weather in Siberia is extremely cold.
	private ['praɪvət]	privat, Privat-	
	planet ['plænɪt]	Planet	
4F	**high school** ['haɪ sku:l]	Oberschule	A school in the USA for kids from 15 to 18
4H	**electrician** [ɪˌlek'trɪʃn]	Elektriker/in	electrician → electrical → electricity
	part-time ['pɑ:t taɪm]	Halbtags-, Teilzeit-	He has a part-time job in the evening.
	practical ['præktɪkl]	praktisch, sinnvoll, vernünftig	practical ↔ theoretical
4I	**bottom** ['bɒtəm]	Ende, (Seite:) Fuß	
	It depends. [ˌɪt dɪ'pendz]	Kommt darauf an.	
	to leave [li:v, left, left]	hinterlassen, dalassen	
	strange [streɪndʒ]	seltsam, komisch	That's a strange story!
5A	**capital letter** [ˌkæpɪtl 'letə]	Großbuchstabe	
	group [gru:p]	Gruppe	
	to compare [kəm'peə]	vergleichen	Compare A with B and C.
	to get back to [ˌget 'bæk tə]	sich melden bei	I'll get back to you in the morning.
	noticeboard ['nəʊtɪsbɔ:d]	Schwarzes Brett	
5B	**since** [sɪns]	seit	It's a long time since I saw Emily.
	regularly ['regjələ]	regelmäßig	
	topic ['tɒpɪk]	Thema	
	classroom ['klɑ:srʊm]	Klassenzimmer	
	gallery ['gæləri]	Galerie	
	walk [wɔ:k]	Spaziergang, Rundgang	
V1	**stopover** ['stɒpəʊvə]	Zwischenaufenthalt, Zwischenstation	The stopover was for two hours.
	competition [ˌkɒmpə'tɪʃn]	Wettbewerb	competition → to compete
	prize [praɪz]	Gewinn, Preis	first prize
	before [bɪ'fɔ:]	bevor	
	to report to [rɪ'pɔ:t tə]	(jdm) Bericht erstatten	
	sight [saɪt]	Sehenswürdigkeit	In the old city there are many sights to see.
	on the way [ɒn ðə 'weɪ]	unterwegs	

Unit 2 People and jobs

	personal ['pɜ:snl]	persönlich	
	personal trainer [ˌpɜ:snl 'treɪnə]	(persönlicher) Fitnesstrainer	
	diet ['daɪət]	Ernährung; Diät	! Aussprache
	healthy ['helθi]	gesund, gesundheitsfördernd	Fruit and vegetables are healthy.
	lifestyle ['laɪfstaɪl]	Lebensweise	
	sports centre ['spɔ:ts sentə]	Sportzentrum	
	hours ['aʊəz]	Arbeitszeiten	She works long hours.
	fit [fɪt]	fit, gesund	
	to keep fit (kept, kept) [ˌki:p 'fɪt, kept, kept]	sich fit halten	She likes to keep fit. She goes to the gym regularly.
1A	**career** [kə'rɪə]	Beruf, Laufbahn, Karriere	a career as a (singer)
1B	**right now** [ˌraɪt 'naʊ]	im Augenblick, gerade	at the moment
1C	**profile** ['prəʊfaɪl]	Profil, Beschreibung, Porträt	
	fitness trainer ['fɪtnəs treɪnə]	Fitnesstrainer	
	outside [ˌaʊt'saɪd]	draußen	Stay here. It's cold outside.
	stadium ['steɪdɪəm]	Stadion	
1D	**inside** [ˌɪn'saɪd]	drinnen	inside ↔ outside
2A	**each** [i:tʃ]	jede/r/s	T-shirts are €5 each.
	to look after [lʊk 'ɑ:ftə]	sich kümmern um, pflegen	He looks after his old parents.
	around [ə'raʊnd]	ungefähr, circa	about

3A	**to interview** ['ɪntəvju:]	interviewen	to interview → an interview
	order ['ɔ:də]	Reihenfolge	in the right/wrong order
	real [rɪəl]	wirklich, ziemlich(, hier:) sehr	
	top man [ˌtɒp 'mæn]	etwa: Spitzenmann	
	in fact [ɪn 'fækt]	eigentlich, um genau zu sein	He's rich, in fact he's a millionaire now.
	mail [meɪl]	Post	
	folks [fəʊks]	Leute	
	barman ['bɑ:mən]	Barkeeper	
	package ['pækɪdʒ]	Paket	A package came for you today.
	crocodile ['krɒkədaɪl]	Krokodil	
	hairdressing 'salon' [ˌheədresɪŋ 'sælɒn]	Friseursalon	
	hunter ['hʌntə]	Jäger	
3D	**kilo** ['kɪləʊ]	Kilo	
	litre ['li:tə]	Liter	
	newspaper ['nju:speɪpə]	Zeitung	Tim reads the newspaper every day.
	Here you go. [ˌhɪə ju 'gəʊ]	Hier, bitte sehr.	
	See you later. [si: jə 'leɪtə]	Bis dann!	
	battery ['bætəri]	Batterie, Akku	My phone battery is empty.
	to phone [fəʊn]	anrufen, telefonieren	
	Darwin ['dɑ:wɪn]	Hauptstadt des Northern Territory	
	beer [bɪə]	Bier	
	ouch! [aʊtʃ]	au!	
	to keep still [ˌki:p 'stɪl]	ruhig halten	
	Watch out! [ˌwɒtʃ 'aʊt]	Achtung! Vorsicht!	
3F	**northern** ['nɔ:ðən]	nördlich, Nord-	northern → north
	southern ['sʌðən]	südlich, Süd-	southern → south
	eastern ['i:stən]	östlich, Ost-	eastern → east
	western ['westən]	westlich, West-	western → west
	life [laɪf]	Leben	life → lives
3F	**population** [ˌpɒpju'leɪʃn]	Bevölkerung, Einwohnerzahl	
	sheep [ʃi:p]	Schaf, Schafe	1 sheep – 2 sheep
	fly [flaɪ]	Mücke	
4A	**to decide** [dɪ'saɪd]	entscheiden	I can't decide. The red one or the blue one?
	to belong [bɪ'lɒŋ]	gehören	This laptop doesn't belong to me.
	salon ['sælɒn]	(Friseur-, Kosmetik-)Salon	
	nursery assistant ['nɜ:səri əsɪstənt]	Hilfslehrerin im Kindergarten	
	busy ['bɪzi]	(viel)beschäftigt	! Aussprache
	to repair [rɪ'peə]	reparieren	
4B	**plant** [plɑ:nt]	Pflanze	I prefer plants and animals to mechanical things.
	ill [ɪl]	krank	
4C	**present continuous** [ˌpreznt kən'tɪnjuəs]	Verlaufsform des Präsens	
	exercise machine ['eksəsaɪz məʃi:n]	Fitnessgerät	
	quiet ['kwaɪət]	ruhig, still	quiet ↔ noisy
4D	**to complete** [kəm'pli:t]	ausfüllen	
	workshop ['wɜ:kʃɒp]	Werkstatt	
4E	**careful** ['keəfl]	vorsichtig	She's a good driver. She's very careful.
	spelling ['spelɪŋ]	Schreibweise, Rechtschreibung	The spelling is wrong. Can you do a spell check?
	to lift [lɪft]	heben, hochheben	
	weight [weɪt]	Gewicht	weight → to weigh
	mechanical [mɪ'kænɪkl]	mechanisch	
	drive [draɪv, drəʊv, 'drɪvən]	fahren	
	nursery (school) ['nɜ:səri sku:l]	Kindergarten	
4F	**to deliver** [dɪ'lɪvə]	(aus)liefern, (Post:) austragen	You order online and they deliver the next day.
	to cut (cut, cut) [kʌt, kʌt, kʌt]	schneiden	cutting

	to hunt [hʌnt]	jagen	
	to serve [sɜ:v]	(Kunden) bedienen, (Speisen) servieren	They serve steak with chips.
	customer ['kʌstəmə]	Kunde/Kundin	The customer is always right!
4G	**kitchen** ['kɪtʃɪn]	Küche	
	chef [ʃef]	Koch/Köchin	A chef works in the kitchen, not in an office!
	to show sb round [ˌʃəʊ 'raʊnd]	jdn herumführen	Let me show you round my house.
	typical ['tɪpɪkl]	typisch, normal	
	to prepare [prɪ'peə]	zubereiten, kochen	At the moment I'm preparing a big meal.
	lamb [læm]	Lamm	
	garlic ['gɑ:lɪk]	Knoblauch	
	sauce [sɔ:s]	Soße	
	colleague ['kɒlɪ:g]	Kollege/Kollegin	
	over there [ˌəʊvə 'ðeə]	dort drüben	Can you see the dark clouds over there?
	meat [mi:t]	Fleisch	
	to get ready [ˌget 'redi]	sich vorbereiten, sich fertig machen	We leave soon. I must get ready.
4H	**postman** ['pəʊstmən]	Postbote	
	to hold (held, held) [həʊld, held, held]	halten, festhalten	Can you hold this package for a moment?
	shorts ['ʃɔ:ts]	kurze Hosen	The shorts are too long.
	foreground ['fɔ:graʊnd]	Vordergrund	foreground ↔ background
	to take off [teɪk 'ɒf]	(Flugzeug:) starten, abheben	to take off ↔ to land
	to describe [dɪ'skraɪb]	beschreiben	
5B	**postwoman** ['pəʊstwʊmən]	Postbotin	
	model ['mɒdl]	Muster, Vorlage	
V2	**visitor** ['vɪzɪtə]	Besucher/in	

Unit 3 Products and services

	product ['prɒdʌkt]	Produkt	
	service ['sɜ:vɪs]	Dienstleistung, Dienst, Service	
1A	**to start** [stɑ:t]	gründen	He started his company many years ago.
	to call [kɔ:l]	nennen, rufen	They called the baby Anne.
	to join [dʒɔɪn]	beitreten, mitmachen	He joined a fitness club.
	billionth ['bɪljənθ]	milliardste/r/s	
	user ['ju:zə]	Nutzer/in	
	billion ['bɪljən]	Milliarde	
	million ['mɪljən]	Million	
1B	**cheat sheet** ['tʃi:t ʃi:t]	Spickzettel	
	above [ə'bʌv]	oben(stehend)	above ↔ below
1C	**to name** [neɪm]	nennen, benennen	Can you name all the planets?
	to follow ['fɒləʊ]	folgen	
	reason ['rɪ:zn]	Grund, Begründung	What's the reason you don't like Facebook?
2A	**article** ['ɑ:tɪkl]	Artikel	
	history ['hɪstri]	Geschichte	
	sneakers ['sni:kəz]	Turnschuhe	
	flat [flæt]	flach	It's flat here. There are no hills.
	to sneak [sni:k]	schleichen	
	athlete ['æθli:t]	Sportler/in, Leichtathlet/in	! Aussprache
	pair [peə]	Paar	a pair of shoes
2B	**simple** ['sɪmpl]	einfach	
	rubber ['rʌbə]	Gummi	
	sole [səʊl]	Sohle	
	canvas ['kænvəs]	Segeltuch	
	top [tɒp]	Oberteil	
	comfortable ['kʌmftəbl]	bequem	comfortable ↔ uncomfortable
	Olympic Games [əˌlɪmpɪk 'geɪmz]	Olympische Spiele	

	fashionable ['fæʃnəbl]	in Mode	fashionable → fashion
	hi-tech ['haɪ tek]	techologisch fortgeschritten	
	air [eə]	Luft	The air in the mountains is clean.
2C	**regular** ['regjələ]	regelmäßig	
	irregular [ɪ'regjələ]	unregelmäßig	
2F	**simple past** [ˌsɪmpl 'pɑ:st]	einfache Vergangenheit	
3A	**public relations** [ˌpʌblɪk rɪ'leɪʃnz]	PR, Öffentlichkeitsarbeit	
	department [dɪ'pɑ:tmənt]	Abteilung	It's a big company, so there are many different departments.
	original [ə'rɪdʒənl]	ursprünglich, original	I still have the original photo.
	to design [dɪ'zaɪn]	entwerfen, gestalten	
	China ['tʃaɪnə]	China	**!** Aussprache
	pharmacist ['fɑ:məsɪst]	(AE:) Apotheker/in	
	lady ['leɪdi]	Dame	
	gentleman ['dʒentlmən]	Herr	
	design [dɪ'zaɪn]	Entwurf, Gestaltung	
	Austria ['ɒstrɪə]	Österreich	
3B	**Atlanta** [ət'læntə]	Hauptstadt Georgias	
	Georgia ['dʒɔ:dʒə]	US-Bundesstaat	
	assistant [ə'sɪstnt]	Helfer/in, Assistent/in	I couldn't do the job without my assistant.
	businessman ['bɪznɪsmən]	Geschäftsmann	
	can [kæn]	Dose	a can of sth
3C	**to invent** [ɪn'vent]	erfinden	Who invented the mobile phone?
	at first [ət 'fɜ:st]	zunächst, zuerst	At first they lost money, then it got better.
4A	**at the back** [ət ðə 'bæk]	hinten	I like to sit at the back of the cinema.
	quietly ['kwaɪətli]	leise	
	village ['vɪlɪdʒ]	Dorf	village – town – city
	race [reɪs]	Rennen, Wettlauf	
4B	**to feel (felt, felt)** [fi:l, felt, felt]	(sich) fühlen	Do you feel well?
	spikes [spaɪks]	Spikes	
	audience ['ɔ:diəns]	Publikum, Zuschauer	The audience laughed.
	cool [ku:l]	cool, dufte	
	to become (became, become) [bɪ'kʌm, bɪ'keɪm, bɪ'kʌm]	werden	When did you become so slim?
	item ['aɪtəm]	Artikel	There are 100 items on the list.
	way [weɪ]	Weg, Art (und Weise)	There are many ways to cook rice.
4C	**fact** [fækt]	Tatsache	
4E	**both** [bəʊθ]	beide/s	Meat or fish? – I like both.
	muesli ['mju:zli]	Müsli	
	orange juice ['ɒrɪndʒ dʒu:s]	Orangensaft	
	text [tekst]	SMS	I can't talk now. I will text you.
4F	**gym** [dʒɪm]	Fitnessklub	
4G	**to translate** [træns'leɪt]	übersetzen	to translate → translation
	camera ['kæmərə]	Kamera	
5A	**invention** [ɪn'venʃn]	Erfindung	invention → to invent → inventor
	mobile phone [məʊbaɪl 'fəʊn]	Mobiltelefon, Handy	
	phone call ['fəʊn kɔ:l]	Anruf, Telefongespräch	
	to produce [prə'dju:s]	produzieren, herstellen	They produce these tablets in China.
	commercial [kə'mɜ:ʃl]	kommerziell	commercial → commerce
	text messaging ['tekst mesɪdʒɪŋ]	Versenden von SMS	
	to weigh [weɪ]	wiegen	How much do you weigh?
	kilogram ['kɪləgræm]	Kilogramm	
	gram [græm]	Gramm	
V3	**scene** [si:n]	Szene	
	to shoot (shot, shot) [ʃu:t, ʃɒt, ʃɒt]	schießen	They shot the film in North Africa.
	leg [leg]	Bein	
	blood [blʌd]	Blut	

	packet ['pækɪt]	Packung	
	hole [həʊl]	Loch	
	clothes [kləʊðz]	Kleider, Kleidung	! Aussprache
	remote control [rɪˌməʊt kən'trəʊl]	Fernbedienung	
	to carry ['kæri]	tragen, mit sich führen	On his last trip he carried 25 kg on his back.
	transmitter [træns'mɪtə]	Sender	
	pocket ['pɒkɪt]	(Hosen-, Hemd-) Tasche	I lost my money. There's a hole in my pocket.
	director [də'rektə]	Regisseur/in	
	to stay [steɪ]	bleiben	I'll stay until the end of the film.
	next door [nekst 'dɔ:]	nebenan	
	unfortunately [ʌn'fɔ:tʃənətli]	unglücklicherweise, leider	It's raining and unfortunately I don't have an umbrella.

Unit 4 Dos and don'ts

	dos and don'ts [ˌdu:z ən 'dəʊnts]	Dinge, die man tun und lassen sollte	
1A	**dental assistant** [ˌdentl ə'sɪstnt]	Zahnarzthelfer/in	
1B	**rule** [ru:l]	Vorschrift, Regel	Do you know the rules for the present continuous tense?
	must not ['mʌst nɒt]	nicht dürfen	You mustn't smoke indoors.
	carefully ['keəfli]	vorsichtig, sorgfältig, gut	
	to have to ['hæv tə]	müssen	You have to smoke outside.
	polite [pə'laɪt]	höflich	polite ↔ impolite
	rude [ru:d]	unhöflich, unverschämt	
	clean [kli:n]	sauber	I need a clean shirt for the party.
	Hygiene ['haɪdʒi:n]	Hygiene, Sauberkeit	
	dirty ['dɜ:ti]	Schmutzig	Hygiene is important in a restaurant. Nothing must be dirty.
	Hard hat [ˌhɑ:d 'hæt]	Helm	
2A	**sign** [saɪn]	Schild	There's a sign on the door.
	car park ['kɑ: pɑ:k]	Parkplatz, Parkhaus	
	construction site [kən'strʌkʃn saɪt]	Baustelle	It's just a construction site now but later it will be a beautiful building.
	smoking ['sməʊkɪŋ]	Rauchen	
	floor [flɔ:]	Boden, Fußboden	There are carpets on the floor.
	electricity [ɪˌlek'trɪsəti]	Elektrizität, Strom	
	lorry ['lɒri]	Lkw	
	driver ['draɪvə]	Fahrer/in	
	bag [bæg]	Tasche, Reisetasche	I left my bag in the taxi!
	fire ['faɪə]	Feuer	
	to transport [træn'spɔ:t]	transportieren, befördern	to transport → transportation
	heavy ['hevi]	schwer	heavy ↔ light
	cell phone ['sel fəʊn]	(AE:) Handy	
	factory ['fæktri]	Fabrik	
	face [feɪs]	Gesicht	With those dark glasses I can't see your face.
	face shield ['feɪs ʃi:ld]	Gesichtsschutz, Schutzmaske	
	no-smoking (area) [ˌnəʊ 'sməʊkɪŋ]	Nichtraucher-	
	volt [vɒlt]	Volt	
	fork-lift truck ['fɔ:k lɪft trʌk]	Gabelstapler	
	wet [wet]	nass, feucht	wet ↔ dry
	goggles ['gɒglz]	Schutzbrille	He wears goggles in the swimming pool.
	ear protectors [ɪə prə'tektəz]	Gehörschutz	
	security [sɪ'kjʊərəti]	Sicherheit	
	property ['prɒpəti]	Eigentum	Houses and flats are property.
	unattended [ʌnə'tendɪd]	unbeaufsichtigt	Parents must not leave their children unattended.
	to report to [rɪ'pɔ:t tə]	sich melden bei	

	caution [kɔ:ʃn]	Vorsicht	! Aussprache
	danger ['deɪndʒə]	Gefahr	danger → dangerous
	case [keɪs]	Fall	
	in case of fire [ɪn ˌkeɪs əf 'faɪə]	im Brandfall	
2C	**to leave (left, left)** [li:v, left, left]	hinterlassen, stehen lassen, zurücklassen	I can't leave my car here.
	to break (broke, broken) [breɪk, brəʊk, 'brəʊkən]	zerbrechen, kaputtmachen, einschlagen	He broke the glass.
2D	**to explain** [ɪk'spleɪn]	erklären, erläutern	Can you explain how it works?
	casual ['kæʒuəl]	leger, ungezwungen	The new boss is very relaxed and casual.
	formal ['fɔ:ml]	formell, förmlich	
	suit [su:t]	Anzug	Men and women wear suits.
	skirt [skɜ:t]	Rock	
	Keep out! [ki:p 'aʊt]	Betreten verboten!	
3	**conflict** ['kɒnflɪkt]	Streit, Konflikt	When people don't agree there is sometimes a conflict.
	news story ['nju:z stɔ:ri]	(aktueller) Artikel, Reportage	
	workplace ['wɜ:kpleɪs]	Arbeitsplatz	
	task [tɑ:sk]	Aufgabe	
	dental practice ['dentl præktɪs]	Zahnarztpraxis	
	reception [rɪ'sepʃn]	Rezeption	
	reception desk [rɪ'sepʃn desk]	Empfang, Anmeldung	
	to answer the phone [ˌɑ:nsə ðə 'fəʊn]	ans Telefon gehen, Anrufe entgegennehmen	
	appointment [ə'pɔɪntmənt]	Termin	I have a dental appointment at 9 am.
	and so on [ənd ˌsəʊ 'ɒn]	und so weiter	
	to share [ʃeə]	(sich etw) teilen	
	dentist ['dentɪst]	Zahnarzt/-ärztin	
	cash [kæʃ]	Bargeld	Do you want cash or a cheque?
	to refuse [rɪ'fju:z]	sich weigern	
	generally ['dʒenrəli]	im Allgemeinen, eigentlich	
	national ['næʃnl]	landesweit, national	
	chain [tʃeɪn]	Kette	They have a chain of shops all over the country.
	angry ['æŋgri]	böse, wütend, verärgert	
	unhappy [ˌʌn'hæpi]	unzufrieden, unglücklich	
	on the other hand [ˌɒn ðɪ 'ʌðə hænd]	dagegen, andererseits	I have work to do. On the other hand, the weather is so nice.
	to clean [kli:n]	säubern, reinigen, putzen	
	to move sth around [ˌmu:v ə'raʊnd]	etw herumtragen, etw herumschleppen	I want to move the furniture in my room around.
3A	**manager** ['mænɪdʒə]	Geschäftsführer/in	
	others ['ʌðəz]	die anderen, andere	Only two people came. The others were busy.
3B	**according to** [ə'kɔ:dɪŋ tə]	gemäß, zufolge, nach	
	to feel (felt, felt) [fi:l, felt, felt]	der Meinung sein, meinen, finden	
	feeling ['fi:lɪŋ]	Gefühl, Meinung, Ansicht	I'm afraid to tell her my true feelings.
	to get angry ['get 'æŋgri]	sich aufregen, sich ärgern	He got angry when I told him the truth.
	to solve [sɒlv]	lösen	I'm sure we can solve the problem.
	boss [bɒs]	Chef/in	
	probably ['prɒbəbli]	wahrscheinlich	He's probably late because of the traffic.
	to put up with (sth) [ˌpʊt 'ʌp wɪð]	etw hinnehmen, sich etw gefallen lassen	There are some things I can't put up with. I'm going!
	discussion [dɪs'kʌʃn]	Diskussion	
	head office [ˌhed 'ɒfɪs]	(Firmen-)Zentrale	
4A	**to smoke** [sməʊk]	rauchen	
	nowadays ['naʊədeɪz]	heutzutage, heute	Nowadays everybody has a mobile phone.
	distance ['dɪstəns]	Entfernung, Strecke	
4B	**office worker** ['ɒfɪs wɜ:kə]	Büroangestellte/r	
	tie [taɪ]	Krawatte	

	to enjoy sth [ɪn'dʒɔɪ]	etw genießen	I really enjoyed the party.
	Coney Island [ˌkəʊni 'aɪlənd]	südl. Zipfel von Brooklyn mit Strand und Vergnügungsparks	
	to relax [rɪ'læks]	sich ausruhen, sich entspannen	to relax → relaxation
4C	**no parking** [ˌnəʊ 'pɑ:kɪŋ]	Parken verboten	
	to park [pɑ:k]	parken	
	lottery ['lɒtəri]	Lotto, Lotterie	
	meeting ['mi:tɪŋ]	Sitzung, Besprechung, Treffen	
	punctually ['pʌŋktʃuəli]	pünktlich	John always arrives at meetings punctually.
	forbidden [fə'bɪdn]	verboten	
	pupil ['pju:pl]	Schüler/in	
	immediately [i'mi:diətli]	unverzüglich, sofort	His dad had an accident. He had to leave immediately.
4D	**Birmingham** ['bɜ:mɪŋəm]	zweitgrößte Stadt Großbritanniens	
	work placement ['wɜ:k pleɪsmənt]	Praktikum	
	description [dɪ'skrɪpʃn]	Beschreibung	description → to describe
	necessary ['nesəsri]	nötig, notwendig	Don't bring flowers. They are not necessary.
	to dress [dres]	sich kleiden	
	smartly ['smɑ:tli]	schick, elegant	He always dresses smartly.
	punctual ['pʌŋktʃʊəl]	pünktlich	
	call [kɔ:l]	Anruf, Telefongespräch	
	to receive [rɪ'si:v]	empfangen, erhalten	to receive ↔ to send
	no-smoking [ˌnəʊ 'sməʊkɪŋ]	Nichtraucher-	
	to ring sb (rang, rung) [rɪŋ, ræŋ, rʌŋ]	klingeln, läuten	The phoning is ringing.
	to turn off [ˌtɜ:n 'ɒf]	ausschalten	to turn off ↔ to turn on
4F	**road sign** ['rəʊd saɪn]	Straßenschild, Verkehrsschild	
	traffic lights ['træfɪk ˌlaɪts]	Ampel	The traffic lights were red.
	speed [spi:d]	Geschwindigkeit	
	speed limit ['spi:d lɪmɪt]	Geschwindigkeitsbegrenzung	
	per [pə, pɜ:]	pro	
	to be allowed to do sth [bi əˌlaʊd tə 'du]	etw tun dürfen	You aren't allowed to smoke in the cinema.
4G	**goods** [gʊdz]	Güter, Waren	They receive the goods from all over Europe.
	in the workplace [ɪn ðə 'wɜ:kpleɪs]	am Arbeitsplatz	
	situation [ˌsɪtju'eɪʃn]	Situation, Lage	
V4	**personal assistant** [ˌpɜ:snl ə'sɪstənt]	persönliche/r Referent/in, Chefsekretär/in	

Unit 5 Success stories

	success [sək'ses]	Erfolg	His first song was a great success.
	patio ['pætiəʊ]	Terrasse	There's a table outside on the patio.
	to ring sb (rang, rung) [rɪŋ, ræŋ, rʌŋ]	jdn anrufen	to call sb, to phone sb
	to earn [ɜ:n]	verdienen	
1A	**to be born** [bi 'bɔ:n]	geboren werden	
	Poland ['pəʊlənd]	Polen	
	plumber ['plʌmə]	Klempner/in	'b' wird nicht ausgesprochen.
	own [əʊn]	eigen	my/your/his own
	building firm ['bɪldɪŋ fɜ:m]	Bauunternehmen	
	employee [ɪm'plɔɪi:]	Angestellte/r	
	successful [sək'sesfl]	erfolgreich	successful at sth
	to move to [mu:v]	nach … ziehen	They left and moved to a new town.
1B	**local** ['ləʊkl]	Lokal-, Orts-, örtlich	! Aussprache
	diagram ['daɪəgræm]	Grafik, Schaubild	
2A	**to be no good** [ˌbi nəʊ 'gʊd]	nichts taugen	good *at* sth

	at the top [ət ðə 'tɒp]	oben	top ↔ bottom
	dyslexic [dɪs'leksɪk]	legasthenisch	
	brilliant ['brɪljənt]	genial, glänzend	He's a brilliant player.
	show [ʃəʊ]	(TV-)Sendung, Serie	
	unsuccessful [ˌʌnsək'sesfl]	erfolglos	unsuccessful ↔ successful
	to open ['əʊpən]	eröffnen	
	normal ['nɔ:ml]	normal, gewöhnlich	! Aussprache
	unemployed [ˌʌnɪm'plɔɪd]	arbeitslos	unemployed → to employ → employee
	to train sb [treɪn]	jdn ausbilden	They trained her to work in our call centre.
	to marry ['mæri]	heiraten	married to sb
2B	**south-east** [ˌsaʊθ'i:st]	Südosten	
	pub [pʌb]	Kneipe	A pub is a place where people drink and talk to friends
	on TV [ɒn ˌti:'vi:]	im Fernsehen	
2E	**present perfect** [ˌpreznt 'pɜ:fɪkt]	Perfekt	
3B	**news** [nju:z]	Nachrichten	Immer Singular: The news ***is*** …
	cookery ['kʊkəri]	Kochen	cookery → to cook → a cook
	cookery course ['kʊkəri kɔ:s]	Kochkurs	
3D	**piece** [pi:s]	Stück	a piece of paper
	clothing ['kləʊðɪŋ]	Kleidung	
4D	**police officer** [pə'li:s ɒfɪsə]	Polizeibeamte/r	
	love [lʌv]	Liebe	
	tense [tens]	Zeit, Zeitform	
4E	**leisure** ['leʒə]	Freizeit	In his leisure time he plays a lot of tennis.
4F	**world champion** [ˌwɜ:ld 'tʃæmpiən]	Weltmeister/in	
	junior high school [ˌdʒu:niə 'haɪ sku:l]	Mittelschule	
	professional [prə'feʃənl]	professionell, berufsmäßig	
	to take part in [ˌteɪk 'pɑ:t ɪn]	teilnehmen an	She takes part in competitions all over the world.
	pro [prəʊ]	Profi	
	world championship [ˌwɜ:ld 'tʃæmpiənʃɪp]	Weltmeisterschaft	
	Japan [dʒə'pæn]	Japan	
	to train [treɪn]	trainieren	
	journalist ['dʒɜ:nəlɪst]	Journalist/in	
	headline ['hedlaɪn]	Überschrift, Schlagzeile	
5A	**screen name** ['skri:n neɪm]	Benutzername, Username	
	to continue [kən'tɪnju:]	fortsetzen, fortführen	Don't stop talking. Please continue.

Unit 6 Work experience

	work experience ['wɜ:k ɪkspɪəriəns]	Berufserfahrung, Praktikum	
	suitable ['su:təbl]	geeignet	a suitable person for the job
	daily ['deɪli]	täglich	Her daily breakfast is always the same.
	volunteer [ˌvɒlən'tɪə]	Freiwillige/r	I'm a volunteer. They don't pay me.
	Good luck! [ˌgʊd 'lʌk]	Viel Glück!	
	to hope [həʊp]	hoffen	
1A	**college of further education** [ˌkɒlɪdʒ əv ˌfɜ:ðər edjʊ'keɪʃn]	berufsbildende Schule	
	advertisement [əd'vɜ:tɪsmənt]	Anzeige	
1B	**ad** [æd]	Anzeige	Auch: advert
2A	**retailer** ['ri:teɪlə]	Einzelhändler	
	ours ['aʊəz]	unsere/r/s	
	knowledge ['nɒlɪdʒ]	Kenntnis(se), Wissen	Knowledge of foreign languages is very helpful.
	telecommunications [ˌtelikəˌmju:nɪ'keɪʃnz]	Telekommunikation(s-)	

	voluntary ['vɒləntəri]	freiwillig	
2B	**placement** ['pleɪsmənt]	Praktikum	
	sales assistant ['seɪlz əsɪstənt]	Verkäufer/in	
	store [stɔ:]	Laden, Geschäft	There are three stores in town.
	pay [peɪ]	Bezahlung, Gehalt	
	cafeteria [ˌkæfə'tɪəriə]	Cafeteria, Kantine	**!** Betonung
3A	**qualification** [ˌkwɒlɪfɪ'keɪʃn]	Ausbildung, Qualifikation	qualification → to qualify
	secondary school ['sekəndri ˌsku:l]	weiterführende Schule	
	foreign language [ˌfɒrən 'læŋgwɪdʒ]	Fremdsprache	
	interest ['ɪntrəst]	Interesse	
	mother tongue [ˌmʌðə 'tʌŋ]	Muttersprache	
3B	**unpaid** [ʌn'peɪd]	unbezahlt	They are only offering unpaid work.
	to provide [prə'vaɪd]	zur Verfügung stellen, bieten	We can provide you with everything you need.
	area ['eəriə]	Bereich	What area do you work in?
	including [ɪn'klu:dɪŋ]	einschließlich	
3C	**to advertise** ['ædvətaɪz]	ausschreiben, annoncieren	
	to attach [ə'tætʃ]	beifügen, anhängen	
4A	**work experience placement** ['wɜ:k ɪkspɪərɪəns pleɪsmənt]	Praktikum	
4C	**travel expenses** ['trævl ɪkspensɪz]	Reisekosten	
4D	**manufacturer** [ˌmænjə'fæktʃərə]	Hersteller, Fabrikant	
	experts ['ekspɜ:ts]	Fachleute	
	programme ['prəʊgræm]	Programm	
	director [də'rektə]	Direktor/in, Leiter/in	
4E	**type** [taɪp]	Art	
	comma ['kɒmə]	Komma	
	repair workshop [rɪ'peə wɜ:kʃɒp]	Reparaturwerkstatt	
4F	**to guarantee** [ˌgærən'ti:]	garantieren	We can't guarantee you work.
4G	**CV = curriculum vitae** [ˌsi: 'vi:]	Lebenslauf	
	to complete [kəm'pli:t]	(Ausbildung etc.:) abschließen	
	education [ˌedjʊ'keɪʃn]	Bildung, Ausbildung	a good education
4I	**to be keen to do sth** [bi ˌki:n tə 'du:]	sehr daran interessiert sein, etw zu tun; etw unbedingt tun wollen	We are keen to get to know you.
	date of birth [ˌdeɪt əv 'bɜ:θ]	Geburtsdatum	
	Yours sincerely ['jɔ:z sɪn'sɪəli]	Mit freundlichen Grüßen	
	primary school ['praɪməri ˌsku:l]	Grundschule	
	skill [skɪl]	Fähigkeit, Fertigkeit	You need skills, not just knowledge.
	chance [tʃɑ:ns]	Möglichkeit, Gelegenheit, Chance	I am looking for a chance to work in another country.
	currently ['kʌrəntli]	derzeit, zurzeit, momentan	We currently have three placements for EU students.
5A	**application** [ˌæplɪ'keɪʃn]	Bewerbung	We received 100 applications.
	to exchange [ɪks'tʃeɪndʒ]	austauschen	They exchanged addresses.
V6	**column** ['kɒləm]	(Text-)Spalte	

Alphabetisches Vokabular

A

above oben(stehend) 41
access Zugang, Zugriff 11
according to gemäß, zufolge, nach 55
actor Schauspieler 12
ad Anzeige 71
administration Verwaltung 25
to advertise ausschreiben, annoncieren 75
advertisement Anzeige 71
air Luft 43
album Album, CD, Schallplatte 13
almost fast, beinah 24
and so on und so weiter 54
angry böse, wütend, verärgert 54
to answer the phone ans Telefon gehen, Anrufe entgegennehmen 54
apartment (AE:) Wohnung 14
application Bewerbung 79
appointment Termin 54
a quarter to (Uhrzeit:) Viertel vor 14
area Bereich 75
around ungefähr, circa 33
around the world auf der ganzen Welt 20
art Kunst, Graphic 25
article Artikel 42
assistant Helfer/in, Assistent/in 45
astronaut Astronaut/in 27
at first zunächst, zuerst 45
athlete Sportler/in, Leichtathlet/in 42
athletics Leichtathletik 22
to attach beifügen, anhängen 75
at the back hinten 46
at the top oben 62
at work bei der Arbeit 17
audience Publikum, Zuschauer 46
automotive mechanics Kraftfahrzeugmechanik 25

B

back Rücken 12
backpacker Rucksacktourist/in 16
bag Tasche, Reisetasche 52
barman Barkeeper 35
battery Batterie, Akku 35
to be allowed to do sth etw tun dürfen 58
bean Bohne 16
beauty Schönheit, Kosmetik 25
to be born geboren werden 61
to be called heißen 9
to become (became, become) werden 46
beer Bier 35
before bevor 29
to be keen to do sth sehr daran interessiert sein, etw zu tun; etw unbedingt tun wollen 78
to belong gehören 36
to be no good nichts taugen 62
between zwischen 20
billion Milliarde 41
billionth milliardste/r/s 41
blood Blut 49
body Körper 12
to book reservieren, buchen 16
boss Chef/in 55
both beide/s 48
bottom Ende, (Seite:) Fuß 28
break Pause 22
to break (broke, broken) zerbrechen, kaputtmachen, einschlagen 52
brilliant genial, glänzend 62
brochure Prospekt, Broschüre 10
building firm Bauunternehmen 61
bus driver Busfahrer/in 16
business administration Betriebswirtschaftslehre 25
business course Betriebswirtschaftslehrgang 22
businessman Geschäftsmann 45
busy (viel)beschäftigt 36
bye tschüs 10

C

cafeteria Cafeteria, Kantine 73
call Anruf, Telefongespräch 57
to call nennen, rufen 41
camera Kamera 48
can Dose 45
canoeing Kanufahren 10
canvas Segeltuch 43
capital city Hauptstadt 17
capital letter Großbuchstabe 29
career Beruf, Laufbahn, Karriere 31
careful vorsichtig 37
carefully vorsichtig, sorgfältig, gut 51
car park Parkplatz, Parkhaus 52
carrot Karotte, Möhre 16
to carry tragen, mit sich führen 49
case Fall 53
cash Bargeld 54
casual leger, ungezwungen 52
caution Vorsicht 53
celeb Promi 12
celebrity Prominente/r 12
cell phone (AE:) Handy 52
certainly gewiss, sicherlich 16
chain Kette 54
chance Möglichkeit, Gelegenheit, Chance 78
cheat sheet Spickzettel 41
to check überprüfen, kontrollieren 10
chef Koch/Köchin 38
child care Kinderbetreuung 25
to choose wählen, auswählen, aussuchen 19
classroom Klassenzimmer 29
to clean säubern, reinigen, putzen 54
clean sauber 51
clothes Kleider, Kleidung 49
clothing Kleidung 65
colleague Kollege/Kollegin 38
college Hochschule, Berufsbildende Schule, Universität 20
college of further education berufsbildende Schule 71
column (Text-)Spalte 69
comfortable bequem 43
comma Komma 77
commercial kommerziell 49
community Gemeinde 20
community college (AE:) College zur Berufsausbildung und Vorbereitung auf ein Hochschulstudium 21
company Unternehmen, Firma 14
to compare vergleichen 29
competition Wettbewerb 29
to complete (Ausbildung etc.:) abschließen 78
conflict Streit, Konflikt 54
construction Baugewerbe, Bauwesen 25
construction site Baustelle 52
construction worker Bauarbeiter/in 8
to contact sich in Verbindung setzen mit 11
to continue fortsetzen, fortführen 69
conversation Gespräch, Unterhaltung 16
cook Koch/Köchin 17
cookery Kochen 64
cookery course Kochkurs 64
cool cool, dufte 46
course Kurs, Lehrgang 22
credit etwa: Leistungspunkte 25
credit card Kreditkarte 16
crocodile Krokodil 35
crown Krone 17
currently derzeit, zurzeit, momentan 78
customer Kunde/Kundin 37
to cut (cut, cut) schneiden 37
CV = curriculum vitae Lebenslauf 78
cycling Fahrradfahren 10

D

daily täglich 70
danger Gefahr 53
date of birth Geburtsdatum 78
to decide entscheiden 36
decorator Maler/in, Tapezierer/in 9

to deliver (aus)liefern, (Post:) austragen 37
dental assistant Zahnarzthelfer/in 51
dental practice Zahnarztpraxis 54
dentist Zahnarzt/-ärztin 54
department Abteilung 44
to depend on abhängen von, ankommen auf 28
to describe beschreiben 38
description Beschreibung 57
design Entwurf, Gestaltung 44
to design entwerfen, gestalten 44
details Einzelheiten, Angaben 25
diagram Grafik, Schaubild 61
diet Ernährung; Diät 30
dining room Esszimmer, Speisesaal 10
director Direktor/in, Leiter/in 77
dirty schmutzig 51
discussion Diskussion 55
distance Entfernung, Strecke 56
doctor Arzt, Ärztin 9
doctor's receptionist Sprechstundenhilfe 9
dos and don'ts Dinge, die man tun und lassen sollte 50
double room Doppelzimmer 18
to dress sich kleiden 57
to drive fahren 37
driver Fahrer/in 52
dyslexic legasthenisch 62

E

each jede/r/s 32
to earn verdienen 61
ear protectors Gehörschutz 52
eastern östlich, Ost- 35
education Bildung, Ausbildung 78
electrical elektrisch 16
electrician Elektriker/in 28
electricity Elektrizität, Strom 52
electronics Elektronik 24
to email eine E-Mail schreiben 25
employee Angestellte/r 61
engine Motor 16
to enjoy sth etw genießen 56
enough genug, genügend 25
entry Zugang 6
etc. usw. 11
euro Euro 16
even sogar, noch 25
everyone jeder, alle 25
exchange Austausch 20
to exchange austauschen 79
exercise machine Fitnessgerät 36
expert Fachmann/-frau 77
experts Fachleute 77
to explain erklären, erläutern 52
extremely äußerst 27

F

face Gesicht 52
face shield Gesichtsschutz, Schutzmaske 52
facilities Einrichtung(en), Räumlichkeiten, Ausstattung 10
fact Tatsache 47
factory Fabrik 52
fashion Mode 14
fashionable in Mode 43
to feel (felt, felt) der Meinung sein, meinen, finden 55
feeling Gefühl, Meinung, Ansicht 55
fire Feuer 52
fit fit, gesund 31
fitness club Fitnessklub 15
fitness trainer Fitnesstrainer 31
flat flach 42
floor Boden, Fußboden 52
to flow fließen 23
fly Mücke 35
folks Leute 34
to follow folgen 41
footballer Fußballspieler/in 12
forbidden verboten 56
foreground Vordergrund 38
foreign language Fremdsprache 74
fork-lift truck Gabelstapler 52
formal formell, förmlich 52
fries (AE:) Pommes 16
from around the world aus der ganzen Welt 17
full-time Ganztags-, Vollzeit- 22

G

gallery Galerie 29
garlic Knoblauch 38
G'day (AustrE:) Guten Tag 8
generally im Allgemeinen, eigentlich 54
gentleman Herr 44
to get angry sich aufregen, sich ärgern 55
to get back to sich melden bei 29
to get ready sich vorbereiten, sich fertig machen 38
to get to know kennen lernen 20
goggles Schutzbrille 52
Good luck! Viel Glück! 70
goods Güter, Waren 58
to go off losgehen 16
to go on holiday Urlaub machen (in) 10
gram Gramm 49
group Gruppe 29
to guarantee garantieren 77
gym Fitnessklub 48

H

hairdresser Friseur/in 25
hairdressing 'salon' Friseursalon 35
to hang out with (hung, hung) mit jdm abhängen, sich mit jdm rumtreiben 26
hard hat Helm 51
to have to müssen 51
headline Überschrift, Schlagzeile 68
head office (Firmen-)Zentrale 55
health Gesundheit, Gesundheitswesen 25
healthy gesund, gesundheitsfördernd 30
heavy schwer 52
Here you go. Hier, bitte sehr. 35
high school Oberschule 27
history Geschichte 42
hi-tech techologisch fortgeschritten 43
to hold (held, held) halten, festhalten 38
hole Loch 49
to hope hoffen 70
horse Pferd 19
hostel Herberge 10
hostel warden Herbergsvater/-mutter 10
hours Arbeitszeiten 31
to hunt jagen 37
hunter Jäger 34
hygiene Hygiene, Sauberkeit 51

I

ill krank 36
to imagine sich etw vorstellen 18
immediately unverzüglich, sofort 56
in case of fire im Brandfall 53
including einschließlich 75
in fact eigentlich, um genau zu sein 34
information Angaben, Information(en) 27
information technology Informationstechnologie 25
inline skates Inline-Skates 13
inside drinnen 31
interest Interesse 74
international international 20
to interview interviewen 34
in the workplace am Arbeitsplatz 58
to invent erfinden 45
invention Erfindung 49
irregular unregelmäßig 43
It depends. Kommt darauf an. 28
item Artikel 46

J

to jog joggen 14
to join beitreten, mitmachen 41
journalist Journalist/in 68
junior high school Mittelschule 68
Just a minute! Einen Moment! 16

K

to keep fit (kept, kept) sich fit halten 31
Keep out! Betreten verboten! 53
to keep still ruhig halten 35

programme Programm 77
project Projekt 20
property Eigentum 52
to provide zur Verfügung stellen, bieten 75
pub Kneipe 63
public relations PR, Öffentlichkeitsarbeit 44
punctual pünktlich 57
punctually pünktlich 56
pupil Schüler/in 56
to put up with (sth) etw hinnehmen, sich etw gefallen lassen 55

Q

qualification Ausbildung, Qualifikation 74
questionnaire Fragebogen 13
quiet ruhig, still 36
quietly leise 46

R

race Rennen, Wettlauf 46
radio station Radiosender 26
ready bereit, fertig 16
real wirklich, ziemlich, (hier:) sehr 34
reason Grund, Begründung 41
to receive empfangen, erhalten 57
reception Rezeption 54
reception desk Empfang, Anmeldung 54
receptionist Empfangsdame, -mitarbeiter 16
to refuse sich weigern 54
regular regelmäßig 43
regularly regelmäßig 29
to relax sich ausruhen, sich entspannen 56
remote control Fernbedienung 49
to repair reparieren 36
repair workshop Reparaturwerkstatt 77
to report to sich melden bei 52
to reserve reservieren 16
retailer Einzelhändler 72
retail services Einzelhandel 25
right now im Augenblick, gerade 31
to ring sb (rang, rung) jdn anrufen 60
road sign Straßenschild, Verkehrsschild 58
rubber Gummi 43
rude unhöflich, unverschämt 51
rule Vorschrift, Regel 51

S

sales assistant Verkäufer/in 73
salon (Friseur-, Kosmetik-)Salon 36
sauce Soße 38
to say 'hello' to sb jdn begrüßen 14
scene Szene 49
scooter Motorroller 13
screen name Benutzername, Username 69
to search suchen, durchsuchen 20
secondary school weiterführende Schule 74
security Sicherheit 52
See you later. Bis dann. 35
to serve (Kunden) bedienen, (Speisen) servieren 37
service Dienstleistung, Dienst, Service 41
to share (sich etw) teilen 54
sheep Schaf, Schafe 35
shoe shop Schuhgeschäft 16
to shoot (shot, shot) schießen 49
shop assistant Verkäufer/in 16
shorts kurze Hosen 38
should sollte/n 16
show (TV-)Sendung, Serie 62
to show sb round jdn herumführen 38
side Seite 12
sight Sehenswürdigkeit 29
sign Schild 52
simple einfach 43
simple past einfache Vergangenheit 43
simple present einfaches Präsens 22
since seit 29
singer Sänger/in 12
single room Einzelzimmer 18
sir mein Herr 18
to sit down sich (hin)setzen 16
site Website 14
situation Situation, Lage 58
size Größe 16
skill Fähigkeit, Fertigkeit 78
skirt Rock 52
smartly schick, elegant 57
to smoke rauchen 56
smoking Rauchen 52
to sneak schleichen 42
sneakers Turnschuhe 42
social sozial 14
social work Sozialarbeit 25
sole Sohle 43
to solve lösen 55
south-east Südosten 63
southern südlich, Süd- 35
speaking am Apparat 10
speed Geschwindigkeit 58
speed limit Geschwindigkeitsbegrenzung 58
spelling Schreibweise, Rechtschreibung 37
spikes Spikes 46
sports centre Sportzentrum 30
sportspeople Sportler 12
stadium Stadion 31
star Star 12
to start gründen 41
state Staat, Bundesstaat 23
to stay bleiben 49
steak Steak 16
to stop anhalten, stehen bleiben, (Motor:) ausgehen 16
stopover Zwischenaufenthalt, Zwischenstation 29
store Laden, Geschäft 73
strange seltsam, komisch 28
subject Fach, Thema 25
subway (AE:) U-Bahn 15
success Erfolg 60
successful erfolgreich 61
suit Anzug 52
suitable geeignet 70
supper Abendessen 15
to surf surfen 17
swimming pool Schwimmbad 11

T

to take it in turns sich abwechseln 7
to take off (Flugzeug:) starten, abheben 38
to take part in teilnehmen an 68
task Aufgabe 54
tattoo Tätowierung 12
technical technisch 26
technician Techniker/in 8
telecommunications Telekommunikation(s-) 73
tense Zeit, Zeitform 67
terrible furchtbar, fürchterlich 13
to test testen, ausprobieren 19
text SMS 48
text messaging Versenden von SMS 49
thanks a lot vielen Dank 16
thanks very much vielen Dank 10
ticket Fahrschein 16
tie Krawatte 56
tip Tipp, Hinweis 15
to (Uhrzeit:) vor 14
toll free (AE:) gebührenfrei 25
top Oberteil 43
topic Thema 29
top man etwa: Spitzenmann 34
traffic lights Ampel 58
to train trainieren 68
trainers Turnschuhe 16
to train sb jdn ausbilden 62
to translate übersetzen 48
transmitter Sender 49
to transport transportieren, befördern 52
travel expenses Reisekosten 76
trick Trick, Kniff 15
truck (AE:) Lkw, Lastwagen 23
truck driver (AE:) Lastwagenfahrer/in, Fernfahrer/in 23
to turn off ausschalten 57
twice zweimal 17
twins Zwillinge 9
type Art 77
typical typisch, normal 38

Entry page 12 – Quiz key

Mats Hummels

1 T
2 F (he plays for Germany and Borussia Dortmund)
3 T
4 F (he does have a younger brother who is a footballer but his name is Jonas Hummels)
5 T

Lady Gaga

6 b
7 c
8 a
9 a

Robert Pattinson

10 T
11 F (he is from London, England)
12 F (his middle names are Douglas Thomas)
13 T
14 T

Factfile: The English-speaking world

		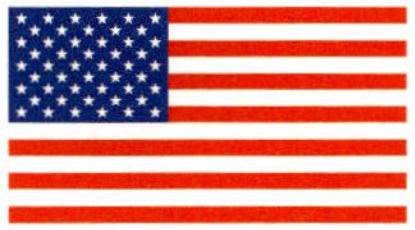			
	United Kingdom (UK)	**The United States of America (USA)**	**Canada**	**Australia**	**New Zealand**
Size (sq. km.)	242,514	9.8 million	9.9 million	7.7 million	270,534
Highest mountain	Ben Nevis (Scotland) 1,343m	Mount McKinley (Alaska) 6,194m	Mount Logan 5,959m	Mount Kosciuszko 2,229m	Mount Cook 3,754m
Capital/largest city	London/London	Washington DC/New York	Ottawa/Toronto	Canberra/Sydney	Wellington/Auckland
Population	60 million (English 84%, Scottish 8%, Welsh 5%, Northern Irish 3%)	300 million (white 67%, black 13%, Hispanic 14%, Asian 4%, Native American 1%)	32 million (81% English-speaking, 19% French-speaking)	21 million (2% Aborigines)	4.1 million (8% Maori)
Top people and parliament	Queen, Prime Minister, *House of Commons*, *House of Lords*	President, *House of Representatives*, *Senate*	Governor General, Prime Minister, *House of Commons*, *Senate*	Governor General, Prime Minister, *House of Representatives*, *Senate*	Governor General, Prime Minister, *House of Representatives*
Important exports	banking, insurance, manufactured goods, chemicals, food	computers, electrical goods, vehicles, food, military equipment, planes	machinery, metals, plastics, wood products, agricultural and fish products	metals, wool, live animals, transport machinery	wool, food and dairy products, wood and paper
Average income (year)	€26,000	€32,000	€25,000	€26,000	€22,000
Money	pound sterling (£)	US dollar ($)	Canadian dollar (C$)	Australian dollar (A$)	New Zealand dollar (NZ$)
Popular sports	football, cricket, rugby	American football, baseball	ice hockey	cricket, rugby	rugby, sailing
Internet domain	.uk	.us	.ca	.au	.nz
International dialling code	+44	+1	+1	+61	+64
Famous people	William Shakespeare, the Queen, David Beckham, Prince William, J.K. Rowling (author of *Harry Potter*)	George Washington (first president), Henry Ford (first mass-produced cars), Neil Armstrong (first man on the moon), lots of film stars!	Avril Lavigne, Alanis Morissette, Keanu Reeves, James Naismith (invented basketball)	Mel Gibson, Nicole Kidman, Kylie Minogue, Rupert Murdoch (started Sky TV)	Peter Jackson (director of *Lord Of The Rings*), Russell Crowe, A.J. Hackett (invented bungee jumping)

Bildquellennachweis

4.1 Getty Images (Digital Vision/Michael Blann), München; **4.2** iStockphoto (Aldo Murillo), Calgary, Alberta; **4.3** Fotolia.com (Victoria Andreas), New York; **4.4** Getty Images (Bloomberg), München; **5.1** iStockphoto (Daniel Laflor), Calgary, Alberta; **5.2** JupiterImages photos.com (Photos.com), Tucson, AZ; **5.3** Thinkstock (Digital Vision/Jack Hollingsworth), München; **5.4** iStockphoto (Kyoshino), Calgary, Alberta; **5.5** shutterstock (George Dolgikh), New York, NY; **6.1** Getty Images (Digital Vision/Michael Blann), München; **6.2** shutterstock (Mat Hayward), New York, NY; **8** Thinkstock (Hemera), München; **8** JupiterImages photos.com (photos.com), Tucson, AZ; **8** Fotolia.com (Goodluz), New York; **8** shutterstock (Tyler Olson), New York, NY; **8** shutterstock (Wavebreakmedia), New York, NY; **9** shutterstock (Andrey Arkusha), New York, NY; **9** iStockphoto (Linda Kloosterhof), Calgary, Alberta; **9** shutterstock (Lisa F. Young), New York, NY; **9** Fotolia.com (Maya Kruchancova), New York; **10** PantherMedia GmbH (Djem), München; **10** iStockphoto (Sun Chan), Calgary, Alberta; **11** shutterstock (Vlad G), New York, NY; **12** Imago (Karina Hessland), Berlin; **12** shutterstock (Joe Seer), New York, NY; **12** dreamstime.com (Featureflash), Brentwood, TN; **14** Thinkstock (Eyecandy Images), München; **14** iStockphoto (Klaas Lingbeek- van Kranen), Calgary, Alberta; **15** Fotolia.com (Goodluz), New York; **17** Thinkstock (iStockphoto), München; **18** Thinkstock (Hemera), München; **20** iStockphoto (Aldo Murillo), Calgary, Alberta; **20** iStockphoto (Kristaps Dislers), Calgary, Alberta; **22** iStockphoto (Aldo Murillo), Calgary, Alberta; **23** shutterstock (Rudy Balasko), New York, NY; **23** iStockphoto (Aldo Murillo), Calgary, Alberta; **24** shutterstock (Piotr Marcinski), New York, NY; **25** shutterstock (Auremar), New York, NY; **28** iStockphoto (Kirby Hamilton), Calgary, Alberta; **29** Klett-Archiv, Stuttgart; **30** Fotolia.com (Victoria Andreas), New York; **30** iStockphoto (Ranplett), Calgary, Alberta; **32** Fotolia.com (Tyler Olson), New York; **33** shutterstock (Nikkytok), New York, NY; **33** iStockphoto (Anne-Louise Quarfoth), Calgary, Alberta; **33** shutterstock (Monkey Business Images), New York, NY; **33** iStockphoto (BlueOrange Studio), Calgary, Alberta; **38** iStockphoto (Susanna Fieramosca Naranjo), Calgary, Alberta; **39** HarperCollins, London-Hammersmith; **40** Getty Images (Bloomberg), München; **40** shutterstock (AHMAD FAIZAL YAHYA), New York, NY; **42** iStockphoto (Eva Serrabassa), Calgary, Alberta; **42** iStockphoto (Cloki), Calgary, Alberta; **42** adidas AG, Herzogenaurach; **44** iStockphoto (Abel Mitja Varela), Calgary, Alberta; **44** Interfoto, München; **44** akg-images, Berlin; **44** Interfoto (Sammlung Rauch), München; **44** Mauritius Images (Alamy), Mittenwald; **44** Picture-Alliance (The Coca Cola Company), Frankfurt; **44** iStockphoto (Robtek), Calgary, Alberta; **45** Corbis (Bettmann), Düsseldorf; **45** dreamstime.com (Mark Williamson), Brentwood, TN; **47** iStockphoto (Kin Yan Chew), Calgary, Alberta; **48** shutterstock (Petrenko Andriy), New York, NY; **49** Picture-Alliance (EPA/PRINCE OF ASTURIAS FOUNDATION/HO), Frankfurt; **49** Klett-Archiv, Stuttgart; **50** Fotolia.com (.shock), New York; **50** shutterstock (CandyBox Images), New York, NY; **50** iStockphoto (Daniel Laflor), Calgary, Alberta; **50** Thinkstock (Brand X Pictures), München; **52** shutterstock (oriontrail), New York, NY; **54** shutterstock (Wavebreakmedia), New York, NY; **57** Thinkstock (Digital Vision.), München; **58** URW, Hamburg; **58** iStockphoto (Compucow), Calgary, Alberta; **59** shutterstock (lightpoet), New York, NY; **59** HarperCollins, London-Hammersmith; **60** JupiterImages photos.com (Photos.com), Tucson, AZ; **60** iStockphoto (Michal Koziarski), Calgary, Alberta; **62** Alamy Images (Allstar Picture Library), Abingdon, Oxon; **62** Picture-Alliance (UPPA/Photoshot), Frankfurt; **64** Thinkstock (iStockphoto), München; **64** shutterstock (Michael Jung), New York, NY; **64** Fotolia.com (Robert Neumann), New York; **65** iStockphoto (Jallfree), Calgary, Alberta; **67** shutterstock (Supri Suharjoto), New York, NY; **68** Thinkstock (Jupiterimages), München; **69** HarperCollins, London-Hammersmith; **70** Thinkstock (Digital Vision/Jack Hollingsworth), München; **70** iStockphoto (Mishkom), Calgary, Alberta; **72** shutterstock (Studio Kwadrat), New York, NY; **73** Fotolia.com (CandyBox Images), New York; **74** iStockphoto (Webphotographeer), Calgary, Alberta; **77** iStockphoto (Sturti), Calgary, Alberta; **79** shutterstock (Andresr), New York, NY; **79** Klett-Archiv, Stuttgart; **80** iStockphoto (Kyoshino), Calgary, Alberta; **82** iStockphoto (Troels Graugaard), Calgary, Alberta; **82** shutterstock (Yuri Arcurs), New York, NY; **82** iStockphoto (Tyler Olson), Calgary, Alberta; **84** shutterstock (Alexander Raths), New York, NY; **84** Thinkstock (Hemera), München; **84** shutterstock (1000 Words), New York, NY; **85** Fotolia.com (Dimitri Surkov), New York; **86** Ullstein Bild GmbH (Granger Collection), Berlin; **87** iStockphoto (Miroslav Georgijevic), Calgary, Alberta; **88** Fotolia.com (Yuri Arcurs), New York; **88** iStockphoto (P_Wei), Calgary, Alberta; **88** iStockphoto (Anthony Seebaran), Calgary, Alberta; **88** iStockphoto (JillKyle), Calgary, Alberta; **88** Fotolia.com (Zhaubasar), New York; **88** shutterstock (Les Scholz), New York, NY; **88** iStockphoto (Flyfloor), Calgary, Alberta; **89** Fotolia.com (WavebreakmediaMicro), New York; **90** Fotolia.com (Robert Neumann), New York; **90** Thinkstock (iStockphoto), München; **92** shutterstock (Wavebreakmedia), New York, NY; **92** Fotolia.com (Sky), New York; **94** iStockphoto (Josef Mohyla), Calgary, Alberta; **94** iStockphoto (Thp73), Calgary, Alberta; **94** Thinkstock (Purestock), München; **95** shutterstock (Wally Stemberger), New York, NY; **95** Thinkstock (iStockphoto), München; **96** iStockphoto (Mark Bowden), Calgary, Alberta; **98** shutterstock (George Dolgikh), New York, NY; **109** Stockbyte, Tralee, County Kerry; **COVER** Thinkstock (Eyecandy Images), München

Sollte es in einem Einzelfall nicht gelungen sein, den korrekten Rechteinhaber ausfindig zu machen, so werden berechtigte Ansprüche selbstverständlich im Rahmen der üblichen Regelungen abgegolten.